Simple Sermons on the Savior's Last Words

Simple Sermons on the Savior's Last Words

W. Herschel Ford

BAKER BOOK HOUSE
Grand Rapids, Michigan 49516

DEDICATED

to

My Precious Christian Friends,

MR. AND MRS. WILL HOLT,

MR. AND MRS. HOSMER W. HILL

MR. AND MRS. A. B. COLEMAN

MRS. SADIE MCMAHAN

and all those who have been so generous in helping to circulate my books of Sermons.

PREFACE

I believe that a man is preaching the Gospel when he centers his thoughts around the Cross of Christ and the Saviour who died thereon. With such thought in mind, I have preached the sermons contained in this book. I deserve no credit for these messages. From many sources and from much reading I have gathered this material. To all from whose writings I have received my inspiration, I give my sincerest thanks.

These are simple sermons which can be easily understood by layman and preacher alike. The Lord blessed their delivery in the First Baptist Church of El Paso, Texas.

My preacher brethren are certainly free to use these sermons in any way which will bring glory to God and souls to the Saviour.

W. Herschel Ford

INTRODUCTION

When you read these beautiful, heart-reaching, simple sermons on the seven last words of our Saviour, you will feel as I felt—an elaborate introduction is out of place. This is sacred ground on which we stand, looking upon the Cross of Him who was made to be sin for us and hearing again His cries of agony, of remembrance, and of triumph.

These sermons were not spun out of a philosopher's chair, far removed from the tears and turmoil of life. They come from the warm soul of a great pastor who lives with his people and who shares with them their daily joys and sorrows. God has wonderfully blest Dr. Herschel Ford with an understanding heart, with a sympathetic spirit, and with a love for the Word that keeps him always close to the Book. He is a Bible preacher in the best and highest sense of the term.

Let me add one other word. You will find in these plain, moving, simple messages the "seeking note." The preacher, like his Master, is after the lost. He is pleading for the soul's return to God. Dr. Ford was converted in a Billy Sunday revival in Atlanta, Georgia. He never gets away from that experience of grace that changed his life and placed his feet on the heavenly road. Dr. Ford is everlastingly the evangelist. I like that. It blesses and encourages my heart.

And may God use these sermons to win others to the crucified One who died that we all might inherit heaven's greatest possession, eternal life.

W. A. CRISWELL

First Baptist Church
Dallas, Texas

CONTENTS

1

"CHRIST'S PRAYER FOR HIS PERSECUTORS"

And when they were come to the place, which is called Calvary, there they crucified Him, and the malefactors, one on the right hand, and the other on the left. Then said Jesus, Father, forgive them; for they know not what they do. And they parted his raiment, and cast lots (Luke 22:33, 34).

Tonight we come to Calvary. CALVARY—the place of curse and the place of blessing. The place of curse for Jesus and the place of blessing for us. CALVARY—where we see man at his worst and God at His best. CALVARY—where the Lamb of God was slain and where the Son of God gave up His life for you and me. CALVARY—where we see the awful depths of human sin and the tremendous heights of divine love. CALVARY—where every man must come if he expects to be saved. CALVARY—where all of our hopes are centered, both for this world and the next.

As we come to Calvary, a hill in the shape of a skull, we see three crosses outlined against the sky. Two thieves occupy the right and left crosses. On the center Cross we see the greatest and best Man who ever lived. Did I say that He was a Man? He was much more than a man—He was God Himself. He had been born in a stable thirty-three years before this time; He had been brought up in Nazareth; He had

11

been baptized at the age of thirty, for three and a half years He had gone about doing good and teaching men the things of God. But these men hated Him, for His own perfect life condemned them.

Now this hate has risen to its most hellish heights. At last Jesus has been condemned. The cry, "Crucify Him!" has been heard in the streets. The long march to Calvary is ended. He has been nailed to the Cross, and that Cross has been lifted up toward Heaven. In fiendish glee His enemies sit and watch Him bleed His life away.

We are interested in the things that men say in the hour of death. Let us lean closer and listen to Jesus. He will say seven important things before He dies. The first statement He makes is this, "Father, forgive them, for they know not what they do." Let us study these words tonight.

I. Jesus' Prayer from the Cross

He was suffering untold agony, He was dying a shameful death. But when He speaks, does He cry out for pity? Does He curse His crucifiers? Does He plead for release? No, He prays, not for Himself, but for all of His enemies. He prayed for those who condemned Him, for those who jeered at Him, for those who nailed Him to the Cross. "Father, forgive them," He prayed. Who else but the Son of God Himself could have prayed such a prayer as that in such an hour as that?

In the original Greek we read that He kept on saying, "Father, forgive them." He prayed this prayer not just once, but many times. When He arrived at Calvary He looked around Him and prayed, "Father, forgive them." When the soldiers crushed Him down and laid Him upon the Cross, He prayed, "Father, forgive them." When the nails tore through His flesh, He prayed, "Father, forgive them." When He was lifted up on the Cross, He prayed, "Father, forgive them." When the crowd jeered Him, He prayed, "Father, forgive them." When the soldiers gambled for His garments, He prayed, "Father, forgive them." No one knows how many times this cry pierced the heavens. He kept storming the Throne of Grace in behalf of others. I want the One who prayed like that to be my Saviour.

His public life began in prayer and now it closes in prayer. What a wonderful example He set! No longer can His hands minister to the sick—they are nailed to the Cross. No longer can His feet run errands of mercy—they are nailed to the Cross. No longer may He instruct His disciples—they have forsaken Him. What, then, can He do? He can pray.

Some people are no longer able to work actively for the Lord. Old age or sickness has laid them aside. In other days they taught the Word of God, they sang His praises, they were active in His service. But now they can do these things no more. They are still in the world, however, and they can still pray. Who knows but that they can do more now than they did in the days of their activity? Maybe God has laid them low that they might become ministers of prayer.

Notice the manner in which He began His prayer— "Father." He showed that He was still conscious of His Sonship. His faith was unshaken by all that He had passed through, by all that He had suffered. They captured Him in the place of prayer, they shifted Him from one unjust trial to another. They stood Him in a corner, they beat upon Him, they spat in His face. They lied about Him, they crowned Him with a crown of thorns, they nailed Him to the Cross. His friends forsook Him. Yet, He still believed that God was on His throne and would do the best thing for Him. He still believed that "all things work together for good to them that love God."

Often when some fine Christian goes through the deep waters of sorrow he is apt to cry out, "Where is God? Why did this happen to me?" But even then we are to remember that He will "never leave us nor forsake us."

> When through the deep waters I call thee to go,
> The rivers of sorrow shall not overflow,
> For I will be with thee, thy trials to bless,
> And sanctify to thee thy deepest distress.

> The soul that on Jesus hath leaned for repose
> I will not, I will not, desert to his foes;
> That soul, though all hell should endeavor to shake,
> I'll never, no never, no never forsake.

In His blackest, deepest hour Jesus' faith shone like a star in the darkest sky. He looked up and said: "Father!" God help us that our faith shall also stand in the hour of trial.

Yes, Jesus prayed on the Cross. His first, fourth and seventh words were prayers. In the beginning, in the middle, and at the end of His agony, His soul was bathed in holy conversation with God.

II. For Whom Did Jesus Pray?

When sorrow comes to us, when it seems that the world is caving in under us, when all help has failed, what do we do? We cry out to God, we reach for the Divine Hand. We say as Peter said when he began to sink, "Lord, Help me." There is nothing wrong with such prayers, for we are invited to come to God in the time of need. But Jesus prayed not for Himself, but for others. He prayed for the soldiers, the religious leaders, the howling mob. Around the bloody shoulders of these murderers He flung the folds of this prayer, "Father, forgive them for they know not what they do."

In this prayer we see the great loving heart of Christ. The text says that "then" Jesus prayed. When did He pray? "Then," when man had done his worst, "then," when wicked men crucified the Lord of Glory, "then," when the devils of earth slew the Lamb of Heaven. It was then that He prayed. Subjected to unspeakable shame, suffering excruciating pain, despised, rejected and hated He was, but then He prayed for those who had brought it all upon Him. Oh, the great loving heart of Jesus!

When Samson died he prayed, "Lord, give me strength to kill my enemies." When Stephen was stoned he caught a little of the spirit of Christ and prayed, "Lord, lay not this sin to their charge." Has someone hurt you in some way? Can you pray for them? If you have the spirit of Christ you will continually pray for them and then some day you may become the best of friends.

A little boy had been quite naughty and his mother had given him a spanking. All afternoon the desire for revenge rankled in his breast. At bedtime he knelt by the bedside and offered his evening prayer. He prayed individually for every member of the family except one. When he arose he looked at his mother with a triumphant look and as he crawled into the bed he said, "I suppose that you noticed you were not in it." But Jesus did not pray like that, He included everyone in His prayer.

In this prayer we see the fulfillment of prophecy. Go back to Isaiah, seven hundred years before Christ, and you hear this prophecy, "He was numbered with the transgressors and bore the sins of many and made intercession for the transgressors." There He is now, seven hundred years later, numbered with the transgressors, bearing the sins of many and praying for those who put Him to death. Everything happened as God said it would happen. In His death Christ thought of His murderers and prayed for them. Oh, blessed Book, which tells us what is going to happen and then pictures it as it happens. Oh, precious Saviour who fulfills every prophecy of the Book.

In this prayer we see Jesus practicing what He preached. One day as He preached on the mountain we hear Him saying, "Love your enemies, bless them that curse you, do good to them that hate you and pray for them which despitefully use you and persecute you." On another occasion He told His disciples that they should forgive seventy times seven times. This meant that they were to forgive without limit. As we hear Him praying, we know that what He preached on the sunny hill of the Sermon on the Mount, He practiced on the grim hill of Calvary.

Is it hard for you to love your enemies, do good to them that hate you, to pray for those who talk about you? Yes, it is. But come to Calvary, look into the face of the One dying upon the Cross, catch His spirit and you will be able to say, "Father, I pray for those who despitefully use me."

We see here also man's greatest need—the need of forgiveness. You may need health, you may need money, you may need friends, you may need an education, but what will all these things amount to if a barrier of sin stands between you and God? Of what use are shoes if you have no feet? Of what use are glasses if you are blind? It matters not how wide a circle of friends you have if you are yet in your sin. It matters not if you have made good in business if your sins are still unforgiven. I know a man who is wonderfully popular—he is probably the best known man in his town—he is fine and clean—he is always ready to do anyone a favor. He has many friends—everyone speaks well of him. But he doesn't know Jesus as his Saviour. One day he is going to die. All of his popularity and his friends and his own kindness will not help him then. The thing that matters most in death is: "Have your sins been washed away in the blood of the Lamb?"

Now, forgiveness from God means more than escaping the penalty of sin. A man murdered another—there was no doubt of his guilt. He was found guilty and sentenced to prison. But he was influential, he had a claim on the governor. It wasn't long until he received a pardon, but the stain of blood was still upon his hands . . . But when you come to Christ and God forgives you, He not only saves you from hell, but He justifies you and makes you as if you had never sinned.

Remember, though you may escape the penalty of sin, you cannot escape the consequences of sin. David in hot blood committed adultery—in cold blood he murdered Uriah. Then the preacher came, saying, "Thou art the man." David, with a voice choking with sobs, clutched God's skirts and cried out, "I am guilty. Oh, Lord, have mercy upon me." God heard his plea and gave him an abundant pardon, but this did not save him from the consequences of sin. He suffered in brokenness of heart until his dying day.

A certain woman swallowed a dose of poison. The preacher came to the hospital to see her. She told him of her bitter experience and said, "I am sorry now. I have sinned. Will God forgive me?" He read to her the precious promises of God and told her that the Lord would forgive her. She accepted Christ as her Saviour. She lingered for a few days, rejoicing that her sins had been forgiven and that she knew the Saviour. But this did not take the poison out of her body and she died in a short time. Yes, if we sin, we must pay for it in some way.

Now, how can we obtain God's forgiveness? The law says that the sinner must die—"The soul that sinneth, it shall die"; "The wages of sin is death." Someone must pay the price of sin—either the sinner or the substitute. Thank God, a Substitute has been provided. "God so loved the world that He gave His only begotten Son." Christ died upon the tree and paid the price for all men. Forgiveness is now freely and eagerly offered to all men, but only those who know that they have sinned and come to Christ confessing their sins can ever receive God's forgiveness.

Here are two men. One is sunk low in sin. He has broken all of God's laws. He has been a burden to others and a blot upon the face of the earth. The other man is a good man—a clean moral man. He pays his debts, he is a patriotic citizen, he is good to his family. We see a difference there, but God says, "There is no difference, for all have sinned and come short of the glory of God." Both must come in the same way to the Saviour and forgiveness and eternal life will be theirs.

So Jesus looked down upon the crowd. Some of them were great sinners, and some of them were small sinners, but He prayed for them all, saying, "Father, forgive them." And isn't this prayer for us, too? Yes, for He says, "Father, I am dying here for all men. When they come to Thee through My shed blood, forgive them." And just as surely as there is a God, He will forgive and save and bless.

III. THE LAST PART OF THE PRAYER

"They know not what they do." Jesus didn't mean that they were ignorant of the fact of the crucifixion. Judas knew that he had betrayed Christ, Pilate knew that he had condemned Him, the mob knew that they had cried out for His blood, the soldiers knew that they had nailed Him to the cross. They knew all this, but Jesus meant that they did not know the enormity of their crime. They knew not that they were crucifying the Lord of Glory.

Yet they ought to have known! He had been prophesied in the Old Testament. Every move of His life fulfilled prophecy. He spoke as never man had spoken before. He lived a perfect life as only God could do. He performed mighty miracles. He went about helping others. Even God had said, "This is my beloved Son." But they were blind; the scales of sin covered their eyes; they did not recognize Him. "He came to His own and His own received Him not."

This same tragedy is repeated today. If you are without Christ you know not what you are doing in neglecting God's great salvation. That's the greatest sin in the world. It is the father of all other sins. You can be forgiven for other sins, but if you go on through life rejecting Christ there is no chance for you. There is nothing left but hell at the end of a Christless life.

This prayer for sinners tells us that no one is beyond the reach of prayer. If Christ prayed for His murderers, then we can be encouraged to pray for the blackest sinners. Do not lose hope, just keep on praying. Maybe someone dear to you is still going on in sin—don't quit praying. Remember the Cross, remember how Jesus prayed for His enemies, and you can surely pray for those whom you love.

IV. WAS JESUS' PRAYER EVER ANSWERED?

Some scholars say that this prayer was a request to the Father asking Him to hold back punishment until these people could know the true meaning of what they were doing. Jesus was saying, "Father, don't strike these poor things down until they have found out what it is all about. They are ignorant now—but they will learn the truth when the Gospel message goes out. Then they will have an opportunity to repent. Give them another chance, Father."

If he had not prayed this way the inference is that immediate doom would have destroyed them. God's wrath would have cut them down. But because of this prayer, they had a chance to be saved.

Yes, this prayer was answered and many were saved. Let me take you to Pentecost. The disciples have gathered together, the Holy Spirit has fallen upon them and Peter is preaching to thousands of people. He told them about the crucifixion and said, "You did this in ignorance." This is what Jesus said. "They know not what they do." When the sermon was ended three thousand were converted. It was not Peter's eloquence that did it, but the Saviour's prayer and the power of the Holy Spirit. On the Cross He prayed that when these people heard the Gospel they might be born again.

You can imagine the scene. When Peter had ended his sermon a man rushed up and cried out, "I clamored for His death—I spat on Him as He passed by. Is there any hope for me?" And Peter says, "Repent and believe and you will be saved." Another says, "I pressed the crown of thorns upon His brow. Is there any hope for me?" Another says, "I slapped His face. Is there any hope for me?" Another says, "I pulled out His beard. Is there any hope for me?" Another says, "I drove the nails through His hands and feet. Is there any hope for me?" Another says, "I lifted up the Cross. Is there any hope for me?" Another says, "I thrust the spear into His side. Is there any hope for me?" And I can hear Peter saying to each of them, "Repent of your sins. Put your trust in the Lord Jesus Christ and you will surely be saved."

Listen, those who crucified Him knew not what they were doing. But you do. You know that He is the Son of God. You know that He went to the Cross for you, that you are a lost sinner, that He invites you to come to Him. You know that you will go to hell if you do not come to Him. You know what you ought to do, why don't you do it? Why don't you come to Christ? Why don't you give your heart to Him and your life to His Church? Why don't you live for Him?

A young man left his home to make his way out in the world. He wasted his money in riotous living, he spent his days in sin and he soon came to the time when he was in desperate need. He appealed to his friends, but they would not help him. At last he wrote a letter back home. "Dear Father," he wrote, "I have been foolish and sinful. I have gotten away from the things that you taught me, but I am sick and I want to get well and live a good life and be the man that you want me to be. I cannot do it without your help. I believe that you love me enough to forgive me and to help me." When the father received that letter, he sped to the side of that son and put all that he had at his son's command. He loved him back to health and helped him to start a new life.

Will a father do that and not the great Saviour who loves you best of all? Oh, He does love you and He will forgive you if you come unto Him. Come tonight and let Him save you. Come and hear Him say: "Thy sins which were many are all forgiven."

2

"CHRIST'S PROMISE TO A PENITENT THIEF"

And he said unto Jesus, Lord, remember me when thou comest into thy kingdom. And Jesus said unto him, verily I say unto thee, to day shalt thou be with me in paradise (Luke 23:42, 43).

Tonight we come again to Calvary. CALVARY—the most sacred place in all the world. CALVARY—where the Son of God died that the sons of men might live. CALVARY—where the rich, red, royal blood of a King was shed for sinful humanity. CALVARY—where the angels wept and the devils rejoiced. CALVARY—where all the sin of the world was laid on the One who had no sin. CALVARY—where men can come and bathe their troubled souls and find the peace which passeth all understanding. CALVARY—where you and I can come and receive life and joy and hope.

In the first sermon Jesus was the only actor in the drama. We heard Him as He prayed, "Father, forgive them, for they know not what they do." Now, two other actors come upon the scene. On either side of Jesus, on the crosses lifted against the sky, hung two thieves. These two were guilty men. These two deserved to die. One plays a minor part in the drama, the other plays a major part as he calls upon the Saviour for salvation. Hear him as he says, "Lord, remember me when thou comest into thy kingdom." Hear the answer of Jesus, "Verily, I say unto thee, today shalt thou be with me in paradise."

I. WE SEE HERE THE CLEAREST PICTURE OF SALVATION BY GRACE IN THE ENTIRE BIBLE

Salvation begins in the heart of God. In his great foreknowledge and election He plans the salvation of the sinner. Before the world began it was His purpose for the thief to meet Christ on the cross in order that the thief might be saved. There are no accidents in a world governed by God. Surely there were none on that day of all days. God was presiding over the scene. From all eternity past He had decreed that all of this would come to pass. Pilate gave the order, "Crucify Jesus between two thieves." He did not know it, but he was putting God's plans into execution. Seven hundred years before Isaiah had said that the Messiah would be "numbered among the transgressors." This was an unlikely thing, that the Holy One who flung the world into space would be dying between two thieves. But it happened just as God said it would.

Throughout His ministry Jesus had been the friend of sinners. His enemies ridiculed Him for it, but He told them that He came to save sinners and not righteous people. "Now," they sneer, "He likes sinners so much, they were His companions in life. We will give Him the privilege of dying with them." And as He hung there between these two thieves, God's first step toward the salvation of one of the men was taken.

Now, the man is in position to be saved. In faith he calls upon the Saviour, and the Saviour promises him a place in Heaven. The man was not good, he did not deserve salvation. It came because of the amazing grace of God. *Ephesians* 2:8—"For by grace are ye saved through faith; and that not of yourselves; it is the gift of God."

Grace planned salvation, grace provided salvation, and grace made this man want to receive salvation. Grace begins and continues and consummates our salvation. If you are saved, if you go to heaven, it will be because of the grace of God. It will not be because of anything that is in you.

This thief had no moral life before conversion—he had no life of service after conversion. Before his conversion he respected neither God nor man—after his conversion he died without having an opportunity to serve Christ. Some people think that we are saved by a moral life, some by the service that we render. But this man had neither of these, so we know that his salvation came entirely through the sovereign grace of God. When we get to heaven, we will not go around saying, "I am here because I lived a good life, I am here because I gave my money, I am here because I served the Lord." Oh, no, throughout eternity we will say, "I am here because I was saved by the grace of God."

The thief's salvation refutes the false ideas of the way that we can be saved today. Some people say, "We are saved by religious ceremony." But this thief was never baptized, he never partook of the Lord's Supper, he never joined a church, he never observed any religious ceremony, he never did any good works. And yet he was saved!

Some say, "You must go to purgatory and burn for a time and then you can enter heaven." But Jesus told this man that he would be in heaven that same day. As a Christian I am not afraid to die, but if I believed that I had to go out and burn for a while in purgatory, I certainly would not welcome death. This record in the Bible does away with the unscriptural and hellish idea of purgatory.

Some people say, "Everyone will be saved." But Jesus did not tell both of these that they would go to heaven. He told only one. Some say, "When you die the soul sleeps until judgment." But Jesus told this man that he would not be forced to wait, but that he would be in heaven with Him that day. Today when a Christian dies, his body disintegrates in the grave, but his real self, his soul, his spirit, goes up to be with Christ. Some say that we are saved by our good character. But this man did not have a good character—his salvation was all of God's grace.

So we see here the great drama of salvation. Jesus is dying for the sins of men—on one side a man is rejecting Him. On the other side a man is repenting and believing in Him. These two men were equally near to Christ. They were both wicked, both suffering, both dying, both of them needed salvation. Yet one rejected Him and died in his sins and went down to hell. The other repented of his sins, believed in Christ, was saved and went up into paradise.

The same thing is going on all over the world today. Christ is presented to two men. One is melted and the other is unmoved. One listens in indifference and the other sees his need and calls for mercy. One turns his back upon Christ and is lost forever—the other trusts Him and is saved forever. Every man has his chance, for God loves every man and wants to see every man saved. But some men will simply not permit Him to save them, and God cannot save them against their wills. The thief upon the cross sets an example for every sinner. He shows how through repentance and faith every man can be saved.

II. HERE WE LISTEN TO TWO DIFFERENT KINDS OF PRAYERS

Did you know that both thieves made requests of Jesus? The first man offered this selfish prayer: "Save thyself and us." The second man prayed, "Stay on the cross, Jesus, and gain a kingdom and remember me when thou comest into that kingdom." The first man simply wanted to be saved from death so that he might live a little longer, holding on to his sins. But the second man wanted to be saved from his sins.

Today a man may come down the aisle professing Christ as his Saviour with the idea only to be saved from hell. Now Christ can and will do that if anyone sincerely trusts Him. But salvation ought to mean much more than that. We ought to be interested in Jesus for His own sake. We ought to love Him and live for Him all of our days.

III. HERE WE LISTEN TO THE PRAYER OF A PENITENT SINNER

"Lord, remember me when thou comest into thy kingdom." This man realized his condition. Wherever there is a sense of God, there is always a sense of sin. As he came close to Christ, as he saw how He acted, as he heard how He prayed for others in His dying moments, he felt himself a sinner. The more vivid our vision of God, the more poignant is our sense of sin. No man ever comes to Christ for salvation until he sees his own lost, sinful condition. Today many men are living clean lives; they are trusting their own righteousness. They do not see their need of Christ. But they will never be saved until they see that their own righteousness can never save them. A man must be abased before he can be exalted. He must be stripped of the filthy rags of his own self-righteousness before he is ready for the garments of salvation. He must come to Christ as a beggar before he can receive the gift of eternal life.

A man must come as a thief before he can find a place in the family of God. But you say, "I am not a thief." Yes, you are, my friend. Suppose that a firm in New York employed a man to represent them in Chicago. Each month they send him his salary check, but at the end of the year they find that he has been serving another firm all of the time, although he has cashed their checks. That man would be a thief. This is the case of every sinner. God sends men into the world. He gives them strength and time and talent to serve and glorify Him, but they serve another master, even the devil. They have robbed God and are just as guilty as the thief on the cross.

This man realized his helplessness. To see ourselves as lost sinners is not enough—we must learn that we are helpless to save ourselves. When we learn that we cannot save ourselves by our own righteousness, when we look outside of ourselves to Christ, then salvation is ours. In the Bible leprosy is a type of sin. Man cannot cure leprosy. Only God can do this. So it is that sin is a dread disease which only God can cure. When the prodigal son realized his need, he went to work, but this did not restore him to his father's house. There was no peace for him until he got up out of his sin and went home . . . A woman came to Jesus one day, bowed down with an infirmity of many years—she had tried many physicians, but she found no cure until she came to the Great Physician. So the sinner tries to save himself in many ways, but he never has his sins forgiven and he never finds peace until he turns his back upon all else and comes to Christ.

What could this thief do to save himself? He could not walk in paths of righteousness for his feet were nailed to the cross. He could not perform any good works for his hands were nailed to the cross. He could not turn over a new leaf and live a better life, for he was dying. All he could do was to call upon Christ. We read these words in *Romans 10:13*—"Whosoever shall call upon the name of the Lord shall be saved."

This man saw the perfection of Jesus. He said to the other thief, "This man has done nothing wrong." God took pains to guard the spotless character of His Son. Judas said, "I have betrayed innocent blood." Pilate said, "I find no fault in Him." Pilate's wife said, "Have nothing to do with this just man." Now the man upon the cross declares that there is nothing wrong with Jesus. It is forever true. He had no sin, but He took our sins upon the tree.

This man recognized Christ's divinity. He called Him "Lord." The Saviour was nailed to the tree. He was an object of hatred. The priests cried, "If thou be the Son of God, come down from the cross." But moved by the Holy Spirit and by faith, this thief owned Christ as divine.

This man saw Jesus as a King. Pilate asked Jesus, "Art thou a King?" Jesus told him that He was. The soldiers made sport of this statement. A king must be properly dressed, so they put a scarlet robe upon Him. He must have a scepter, so they placed a reed in His hand. He must have a crown, so they crushed a crown of thorns down upon His brow. As He hangs upon the Cross now, He does not look like a king, does He? Instead of sitting upon a throne, He is hanging upon a Cross. Instead of wearing a royal diadem, He is wearing a crown of thorns. Instead of being waited upon by a retinue of servants, He is numbered among the transgressors. Yet, in spite of all this, the thief saw Him as a King who would soon inherit a Kingdom. That was not all, however. The thief also saw Him as a Saviour. When He said, "Remember me," he was simply saying "Save me." He surely believed that Jesus was the Saviour for the chief of sinners, or he would not have believed that Jesus could save him. Listen, friend, if Jesus could save a thief while He was dying upon a cross, He can save you.

This man expressed a belief in a future life. He knew that out there somewhere there was a place where God punished sin and rewarded faith. He knew that death on the cross did not end all. He saw Jesus standing out there, a King in a Kingdom, and he wanted to be with Him. Death does not end it all for us, either. "It is appointed unto man once to die, and then the judgment." Whatever your excuse may be now for not living for Christ, let me tell you that one day you must face the judgment and you ought to get ready for it.

A man can realize his lost condition, he can believe in the deity of Christ, he can believe in a future life, and still be lost. What else must he do? The Bible tells us it is "repentance toward God and faith toward the Lord Jesus Christ." The thief exercised repentance and faith and was saved. At first he joined the others in reviling Christ. Now his conscience is stirred up and repentance is born in his heart. He sees God as a Judge, for he said, "We deserve to be dying here. We are receiving our due reward. We must face God." He acknowledges his guilt. He passes the sentence upon himself. He makes no excuses, but he recognizes himself as a transgressor who deserves to die. Every sinner, to be saved, must take his place as a sinner before God; he must acknowledge his sin and must have a

Godly sorrow over his sin. His repentance must then be accompanied by faith in the Lord Jesus Christ.

Jesus was dying upon a Cross. To all outward appearance, He had lost the power to save anyone. His enemies were triumphing over Him, His friends had forsaken Him, public opinion was against Him. No one pointed to Him and exclaimed, "Behold the Lamb of God which taketh away the sin of the world." He looked like a dying Man and nothing else. But in spite of all this the thief took this suffering, bleeding, dying Man as his God. This was real faith, faith kindled in his heart by the Holy Spirit. We note that he did not say, "Remember me *if* you come into your kingdom," but "remember me *when* you come into your kingdom." He showed real faith that Christ, though dying, would some day be King of kings and Lord of lords.

We notice also the humility of the man. James and John on one occasion said, "Give us the chief places when thou comest into thy kingdom," but the poor thief did not ask to be honored or exalted. He simply asked Jesus to remember him. The public soon forgot this man; his friends and his family were glad to forget him; but he wanted Jesus to remember him. He is the One we want to remember us, also. Others may forget us, but if Jesus remembers us that is enough. If you come to Him, He will remember. You will become a part of Him and He will never, never forget you.

IV. Listen to Jesus' Answer, "This Day Shalt Thou Be with Me in Paradise"

Jesus might have said, "You deserve your fate. You are a wicked robber and you ought to die." He might have said, "You have waited too late—you should have come to Me sooner." But He *couldn't* say this. On another occasion He had said, "Him that cometh to

Me, I will in no wise cast out." This man came and now Jesus *must* receive him. There is one thing that God cannot do—He cannot break His promise. Whoever you are, however deep into sin you have gone, if you will call on Him as did the thief, He will receive you and give you a place in heaven.

Jesus is making a direct statement when He says, "This day shalt thou be with me in paradise." Some people who believe in baptismal regeneration say that Jesus was here asking the thief a question. Now, Jesus never said a foolish thing. It would have been foolish if, when the man had prayed, "Lord, remember me," Jesus had asked him the question, "Are you going to be with Me in paradise?"

The Lord always gives us more than we ask. This man simply asked to be remembered. But Jesus said, "I will not only remember you, I will take you with me today to a land where you will never suffer again, and where all of your troubles and tears will be gone forever." When a sinner comes to Christ, not only are his sins forgiven, but the Holy Spirit indwells him, God walks with him, He answers his prayers, He comforts him in sorrow, He stands by him in death and finally takes him up to glory . . . When Christ went home to heaven He had a trophy to lay at the feet of the Father. His trophy was the thief who trusted Him upon the cross. Since that time millions have come to Christ and He has taken them through the fires of earth and hell and has carried them safely home to heaven.

Jesus said, "Thou wilt be with me." He meant not for a month, not for a millennium, but for an eternity. Salvation means eternal union with Christ! Salvation is a Person before it is a place. He is saying here to the thief, "Since you have taken Me as your Saviour, you and I will be together throughout all eternity." Paul looked forward to this time and said, "I have a desire to depart and be with Christ, which is far better than anything that this world can give." You are going to spend the rolling years of eternity somewhere. Do you want to spend them with the devils in hell, or with Jesus in heaven?

An old military officer had had many wonderful experiences. The people who met him loved to hear him talk about these experiences. However, when he had finished telling of some of these experiences, he would say, "But someday I expect to see something more wonderful than all of these things." He was seventy years of age, and they knew he would never travel again. "What do you expect to see?" they would ask him. "The first five minutes after death I expect to see many things far more wonderful than these which I have described." The old man was right. When you and I cross Jordan and see the Lord Jesus Christ, that will be a far more wonderful sight than anything we can ever see in this world.

Jesus told the thief that he would be saved immediately. He did not have to go through a probation period nor through the fires of a purgatory. As soon as he died he entered paradise. The very moment you trust Christ, that very moment you are saved. You are on the way that leads to heaven and the very moment you die, your soul will wing its way to the Glory Land.

The thief had a chance to be saved in the last hours of his life. This was his only chance and he took it. You have a chance to be saved now. You ought to make good your opportunity. In your last hours you may not have this chance. The Bible all the way through rings out with this note: "Now is the time—tomorrow may be too late."

Jesus hung on the tree. His hands and feet were nailed to the Cross. Yet even then He had the power to save a soul from death, open the gates of Heaven, and take the saved man in with Him. If a dying Saviour can do that, how much more can this One who rose from the dead, and who lives forever at the right hand of God! All you need to do is to come as the thief did, take Christ as yours and He will never leave you nor forsake you.

Some day because of the matchless grace of the Lord Jesus Christ I hope to go to Heaven. I will walk down the street and stop at the thief's mansion. I will say to him, "Will you tell me all that happened at Calvary?" Then he will answer, "I will be glad to tell you. I never get tired of telling the story. I lived a sinful life and when the end came, there I was dying upon the cross. Then I looked up and I saw Jesus by my side. I knew that He was more than a man. Hope leaped up in my heart and I cried out, 'Remember me when thou comest into Thy kingdom.' He answered, 'This day shalt thou be with Me in paradise.' When He said that I forgot that I was a criminal, I forgot the cross, I forgot that I was dying. I hung there with a song in my heart, rejoicing that I was going to be with Him in paradise. At three o'clock it was all over. He brought me up here and I have been here ever since. In these two thousand years I have never been able to tell Him how much I love Him."

Then I will say, "Thief, I never saw Him as you did, but I did see Him by faith. He saved me, too. He brought me safely home. I love Him, too." Then we will go down the street together and meet the Saviour and try again to thank Him for saving such sinners as we were. If you are not on the way to heaven, come tonight in simple faith to Jesus and He will save you.

3

"CHRIST'S PROVISION FOR HIS MOTHER"

> When Jesus therefore saw his mother, and the
> disciple standing by, whom he loved, he saith unto
> his mother, Woman, behold thy son! Then saith he
> to the disciple, behold thy mother! And from that
> hour that disciple took her unto his own home
> (John 19:26, 27).

Tonight we come again to Calvary. CALVARY—
where all the rivers of prophecy come together in a
sea of fulfillment. CALVARY—where the blood for our
cleansing was drawn from Immanuel's royal veins. CAL-
VARY—where sinners plunged beneath that flood lose
all their guilty stains. CALVARY—where all the ransomed
church of God is saved to sin no more. CALVARY—
about which in a nobler, sweeter song we'll sing through
the endless ages. CALVARY—where a dying Saviour
invites all men to come and find the life that never
ends.

Jesus spoke seven times from the Cross. His first
word was a prayer to God, asking Him to forgive His
enemies. His second word was a promise to a dying
thief. Tonight we hear Him speaking to His mother
and to John, the beloved disciple. To His mother He
says, "Behold thy son," and to John He says, "Behold
thy Mother." But we must remember always that it was
not the thief, not John, not Mary, but Jesus who was
the central figure in Calvary's drama.

34

Let us picture the scene. Three heavy-laden crosses stand upon Calvary's hill. Jesus, the Son of God, hangs upon the central Cross. The mob jeers, the soldiers gamble, the religious leaders rejoice. Jesus looks down and sees His mother standing near the Cross. By her side is the disciple John. We do not know how close they were, but the Scripture tells us that they were "by the cross." Jesus now lifts His voice and says to His mother, "Woman, look at John. From now on he will be your son." Then He spoke to John, "John, from now on she is to be your mother." Then we are told that from that hour John took her to his own home.

I. THE MOTHER BY THE CROSS

"Now there stood by the cross of Jesus his mother." Mary could have truly been called "the woman of sorrows." When she was just budding into young womanhood, the angel Gabriel came down one day and stood before her. "God has highly favored you," said Gabriel. "He has selected you to become the human instrument through whom His son will come into the world. You are going to bear a child, his name will be called Jesus, he will do mighty things and reign forever and ever." Mary was puzzled and troubled. "How can this be?" she asked. "I am not married, I have had no relationship with any man." Gabriel said, "The Holy Spirit will be the father of this child, and God will speak Him into existence. Don't worry about it, just leave the matter entirely with God."

Mary bowed her head in beautiful submission, "I am the handmaiden of the Lord, be it unto me according to thy words." Naturally she was troubled, however. Never before had a virgin borne a child, never before had a child been born without a human father. She knew that others would not understand. They didn't. In a little while she became the victim of cruel gossip. She was pure as the driven snow, but they spoke evil things about her and it broke her tender young heart.

Yet the young man, Joseph, loved her. He wanted to protect her and was willing to hide her away. Then the angel appeared unto him and said, "Don't be afraid to marry Mary, Joseph. This Child is of the Holy Ghost. Thou shalt call His name Jesus, for He shall save His people from their sins." Joseph went right out and married Mary in spite of the gossip and the wagging tongues. The Scripture plainly tells us that there were no marital relations until after Jesus was born . . . Mary had a cross to bear, but surely in the hours of her despondency she was comforted by saying, "I know that I am doing the will of God. I know that Joseph loves and cares. I will not be hurt by what others say."

The time came when the baby was to be born. They could not find a place in a hotel room or a hospital ward. He was born in a stable, wrapped in swaddling clothes, and laid in a manger. Before long Herod went out to kill all the babies two years of age and under. Joseph and Mary and Jesus were forced to flee into a foreign country, returning later to Nazareth. As Jesus grew up and entered the ministry, Mary saw Him despised and rejected, hated and persecuted. Now she sees Him hanging upon a Cross, dying, and her heart breaks with sorrow.

But hadn't all this been predicted? Yes, when Jesus was but a few days old Mary and Joseph brought Him to the temple to present Him to the Lord, according to Jewish custom. An old man of God was there, Simeon by name. When he saw the child Jesus, he took Him in his arms and prophesied concerning Him. Then He turned to Mary and said, "A sword shall pierce through thy own soul, also."

Now, the prophecy is fulfilled, the sword is piercing her soul. She was the first one to plant a tender kiss on His brow—now that brow is crowned with thorns. She had held the little hands as He took His first steps —now those hands are nailed to the Cross. She had guided the little feet in the right ways—now they are nailed to a tree. Surely Mary wept bitter tears, and her poor heart broke. She remembered the words of Simeon and knew that the prophecy had been fulfilled. She had great bliss at the birth of Jesus; she had great sorrow at His death.

We see here, also, the constancy of a mother's love. His disciples deserted Him, His friends forsook Him, His nation rejected Him, His enemies cried out for His blood, but His mother stood there at the foot of the Cross. The crowds mock Him, the priests jeer at Him, the soldiers are callous and indifferent. Jesus is bleeding to death, but there is His mother, beholding it all. She did not faint, she did not run away, she was bound to Jesus by the golden chains of love, and so she stood there loyally by the Cross. Oh, what faithfulness, what love, what courage!

Today our Catholic friends place Mary in an exalted position never given her in the Bible. They say that Mary had no other children except Jesus, but we read in *Mark 6:3*—"Is not this the carpenter, the son of Mary, the brother of James, and Joses, and of Juda and Simon? And are not his sisters here with us? And they were offended at Him." Here we are given the names of four brothers and at least two sisters. How can we deny the Bible by saying that He had no brothers or sisters?

The Catholics call her the "Queen of Heaven and Mother of God." They insist that she is the mediator between us and Christ. They say that if we want Jesus to hear our prayers we must go to His mother and ask her to intercede for us, because a mother can get her son's ear better than anyone else. Well, Jesus said much about praying, but He never once mentioned Mary in connection with prayer. He told us that the way to get to the Father's heart was through Him. Listen to *I Timothy 2:5*—"For there is one God, and one Mediator between God and man, the man Christ Jesus."

The Bible tells us that Jesus is our Mediator and not Mary. It tells us that our prayers are to be offered in His name, not in Mary's name. When He died upon the Cross, He opened a way for us to go through Himself straight to the heart of God. He does not need Mary's help and neither do we.

We notice in addressing her, that He called her not "Mother," but "Woman." Nowhere in the gospels do we hear Him calling her mother. It was always "Woman." Why did He do that? Surely He must have looked down the centuries. He must have seen the false system which would be built around Mary, therefore He did not use one word to approve such idolatry. Anyone is radically wrong when they render to Mary the homage due only to Christ.

On the Cross Jesus actually broke the relationship of mother and son. He turned her away from Himself by saying, "From now on not I, but John, is to be your son." From that time He is no longer anyone's son— He is the world's Saviour. Mary no longer is the mother, she is a simple believer, and her Son has become her Saviour. Jesus never set her on a high pedestal. She was just another human being, a sinner saved by grace. She was a good woman and God used her as an instrument to bring His Son into the world. But she was still just a human being, and does not deserve the worship offered to her even today.

After the resurrection, she took her place among the other worshippers. It was not a special place—she was just one of the 120 who met on the day of Pentecost. She found the salvation relationship higher than the family relationship. She found it better to have Jesus as Saviour and Lord than to have Him as a son. As a son He made provision for her to stay with John— as a Saviour He said, "I go to prepare a place for you." He provided for her as a Saviour a million times better home than He provided for her as a son.

II. THE SON ON THE CROSS

Probably at this time Joseph was already dead and the other sons estranged from Mary. It is possible that they could not go along with her in the faith which Jesus taught. So Jesus wants to care for Mary's future before He dies. He says to Mary, "Go with John and be a mother to him." To John He says, "Take her and be a son to her." Jesus lived a complete life. He discharged every obligation to God and man. He was not willing to die and leave anything undone that He ought to do. So He arranged for His mother's future.

Here we see Jesus setting a wonderful example. When God gave the Ten Commandments, He gave us instructions as to how we should feel and act toward our parents. *Exodus 20:12*—"Honor thy father and thy mother; that thy days may be long upon the land which the Lord thy God giveth thee." *Ephesians 6:1-2* —"Children, obey your parents in the Lord; for this is right. Honor thy father and mother which is the first commandment with promise."

Now if we honor our parents, we give them more than mere obedience . . . we give them our love and affection, our gratitude and respect. When we are children we are to obey our parents—when we grow

up, although they no longer command us, we are still
to honor them. I remember a certain rich man who out-
wardly claimed to love his mother a great deal. Yet
he allowed other members of the family to keep her
and support her in her old age. He never contributed
to her support, although he was easily able to afford
it. This is not honoring parents.

I believe that a beautiful relationship existed between
Mary and Jesus. Their home was a godly home where
they prayed and studied the Word of God. They at-
tended the synagogue and brought the Lord's tithe to
the church. Now as Jesus dies on the Cross, He shows
a sweet and tender solicitation for her. He gives her a
new home and a new son.

Are you taking Jesus as your example in the matter
of caring for your parents? We can never fully discharge all of our obligations to them. Are you truly
honoring your father and mother? Maybe you are young
and headstrong and you think your parents are old-
fashioned because they do not let you have your way. I
read an article the other day about a teen-age boy who
killed his mother and brother because they would not
let him have the family car.

We must remember that our parents have had wider
experience than we have had. They know the pitfalls
ahead—they know what is best. They are only trying
to do the thing which is best for you. If they deny
you things, it is not because they love to see you suffer
—they are taking the long look—they feel that they
are doing the thing which will ultimately make you
happy. It may not seem that way to you now, but
some day you will understand. If your parents are poor,
you ought to care for them. If they are sick you ought
to minister unto them. If they live in another place,

you ought to write to them often and keep them posted on every detail of your life.

Here is another thought—in serving God, we must not ignore family ties and responsibilities. Of course, if God calls you to serve Him and your parents try to prevent this, you must step out and do what God says. But we must always remember our parental obligations. Here is Jesus doing the greatest thing that was ever done upon this earth—dying for sinful humanity. Yet, He doesn't overlook His responsibilities. He takes care of His mother.

Jesus always did the right thing. No one could ever justly criticize Him. Now no one could ever say He had neglected His mother. Satan cannot accuse Him before God. Even in the darkest hour of His life Jesus could stop dying long enough to do the right thing about His mother. If any man is too busy, even in the Lord's work, to discharge his obligation to his family, let him look to Jesus on the Cross, and remember the example which He set.

Of course, there are too many people who go too far in the other direction. They give all of their time to their home and family and leave God and the church out. That is wrong. But there is a happy medium. Let Christ and His Church and your family have your love and service. Surely all of these put together make the ideal combination.

III. THE DISCIPLE AT THE CROSS

The people closest upon earth to Jesus were His disciples. His life and theirs were knit together by cords of love. But none of them loved Him more than John. In the gospel which he wrote, John refers to himself as "the disciple whom Jesus loved." He loved Jesus, and Jesus loved him. At the last supper, when Jesus sat at the table with the disciples and told them that He was going to die, where do you find John? He was leaning upon the bosom of Jesus. None of the others seemed to resent this—they seemed to realize that John had the greatest capacity for love.

When Jesus foretold His death, He gave a warning to His disciples. He told them that when the Shepherd would be smitten, the sheep of the flock would be scattered abroad. Peter jumped up and cried out, "Though I be put to death with you, I will never deny you." Then we read that *all* the other disciples said the same thing. Now, what did happen? Just what Jesus foretold. *Matthew 26:56*—"They all forsook him and fled."

In a few minutes Jesus stood before the High Priest. The High Priest questioned Him about His disciples. He must have said, "If you are all that you claim to be, where are your disciples? Why have they forsaken you in this hour?" Jesus made no answer. His heart was evidently aching because of sorrow over their leaving Him in the hour when He needed them most. But before you censure the disciples, think of yourself. Have you always been true to Jesus? In the hour of testing have you always stood firm? Have you been willing to suffer shame and disgrace for the sake of Christ?

Now the picture takes on a brighter hue. One of them did return, one of them was brave enough to come to the Cross. And who was it? Was it big, brave Simon Peter, who swore that he would never forsake Jesus? No, it was John, the beloved. His heart of love overcame his fear and brought him to the Cross . . . John was a backslider. A backslider is one who trusts and loves Christ, but who drifts away from Him, sometimes even into open sin. Thank God, John came back. He could not help it. He did love Jesus, he was miserable away from Him. So he came back and stood near the Cross, his heart breaking all the while.

Am I speaking to one who has wandered away from Jesus? Have you lost the sweet communion which once you had? I beg you to come back. He will not rebuke you—He did not rebuke John. Come back to Christ, for the only happy life you can ever have is at His side.

Now when Jesus told John to be a son to His mother, He was simply saying, "I want you to take My place and do My work for Me." That is just what He says to every believer. "Take My place, live My life over, do My work. As the Father hath sent me, even so send I you." Someone has said that the word "Christian" means "a little Christ." You can never do the great things He did, but you can try in your own small way to live as He did and to do His work on earth.

I want you to look at the wisdom of Christ's choice. He knew that John loved Him greatly, therefore he would be the best one to look after His mother. If we love Him, we will look after His interests here. The thing closest to His heart is His church, and its mission of winning lost souls . . . But He was also wise in selecting Mary to be with John. One day on the Isle of Patmos, God would pin back the curtain of eternity and permit John to look into the future. He would then write the Book of Revelation. The best training John could have would be daily companionship with Mary, the woman who lived so close to Jesus in the thirty years before He entered the ministry. Yes, Jesus Christ does all things well.

Before long, all is over. The figure on the central Cross is still. The suffering is over, death has come, death in your place and mine, death which makes men forever more alive. We see John obediently taking Mary to his own home, as Jesus requested . . . A great artist has painted a wonderful picture, showing the three crosses outlined against the evening sky. John is leading Mary away. You can see the agony of her soul in her face. And in her trembling hand she is carrying something. What is it? It is the crown of thorns, taken from the brow of Jesus. We do not know that this is a true picture, but surely this is just like a mother's love.

My friends, Jesus has told us to do certain things, also. Our task today is to live for Him and make Him known to others. Would God that we were as faithful and obedient as Mary and John were!

Yes, Jesus on the Cross remembered Mary, but He also remembered you and me. He gave His life to save us. However, all that He did is in vain as far as you are concerned unless you repent of your sins, open up your heart, and let Him come in and save you.

A preacher went to see a man and said to him, "I want to talk to you about your soul's salvation." The man replied, "I am too busy to talk right now." The preacher took him by the hand, pulled him down close to himself and whispered in his ear, "What if I had been death?" If death came for you tonight, would you be ready? "Believe on the Lord Jesus Christ and thou shalt be saved."

4

"CHRIST'S CRY FROM THE DEPTHS OF SORROW"

> Now from the sixth hour there was darkness over all the land unto the ninth hour. And about the ninth hour Jesus cried with a loud voice, saying, Eli, Eli, Lama Sabachthani? That is to say, My God, My God, why hast thou forsaken me? (Matthew 27:45, 46).

Tonight we come back again to Calvary. CALVARY —where a Saviour died and salvation was born. CALVARY—where God prayed and a mob cursed. CALVARY —where deep darkness enveloped the earth that a divine light might fill the earth. CALVARY—where God's Son was forsaken that we might never be forsaken. CALVARY——where by faith we received our sight and had our burdens rolled away. CALVARY—your hope and mine for time and eternity.

Christ is hanging on the Cross. He has prayed for His persecutors, He has promised life to a thief, He has made provision for His mother. Now the scene changes. Several hours have passed by. From twelve noon until three o'clock in the afternoon darkness has covered the land, hiding from the eyes of man the form of the Son of God. This darkness was a miraculous thing—it was from God. It probably brought silence to the crowd. A strange fear filled their hearts and the only noise that could be heard was the occasional groan of the three victims . . . Then suddenly,

45

like a sharp clap of thunder, a cry rends the heavens. Jesus cried out: "My God, my God, why hast thou forsaken me?" The crucifixion was the most unusual thing the world ever looked upon—this cry was the most startling utterance of it all.

I. Jesus Was Actually Forsaken

These words which He spoke were taken from Psalm 22. Some say that He learned this psalm as a boy and that now on the Cross He was delirious and babbled out these words. Certainly they are wrong—Jesus was perfectly lucid every minute. Some say that He was in such pain that these words were forced from His lips. That certainly could not be so—Jesus gladly laid down His life and gladly endured all the pain for you and me. He had no dread of the physical suffering. Some say that Jesus just "felt" that He was forsaken. No, He knew what it was all about. It was not a matter of feeling with Him, but of actuality. He did not say, "Lord, it seems that you have forsaken me after all." He said, "Thou hast forsaken me."

Jesus was the perfect Son of God. No one ever found any fault with Him, no one could ever truthfully say that He ever did one wrong thing. After twenty centuries have passed we still look upon Him as the One Perfect Man. He was more than that, He was God-Man. Even God added His strongest testimony when He said, "This is my beloved Son." Now why should He ever be forsaken?

He had always been the object of His father's love, even from all eternity past. He was God's only begotten. God the Father loved Him greatly and He loved God the Father with a mighty love. He shared God's glory before the world began—He lived in the Father's bosom. God sent Him into this sinful world, away from heaven, but the fellowship was never broken. For thirty-three years He had an unbroken communion with God. Every thought that He had was in harmony with God's mind—every thing He did was in accordance with God's will, but now on the Cross He cries out, "My God, my God, why hast thou forsaken me?" He was actually forsaken.

There is no sadder word than the word "forsaken." I see a man deep in trouble—he looks around for his friends, and they have all forsaken him. It breaks his heart. I see a wife, sick and helpless and poor—the husband who promised to stand by her forever is gone. She weeps because she is forsaken. I see a little child, wandering through an empty house, tears flowing down her cheeks, hungry and cold and dejected. Her parents have forsaken her. But, oh, to be forsaken of God —to have God turn His back upon you in the darkest time of need! This is what happened to Jesus, our Saviour.

Now Jesus knew what it was to be forsaken. The members of His family forsook Him—His home town forsook Him—the nation He came to save forsook Him. But God never had forsaken Him. Every minute of His life He could reach out and touch God. When troubles came He slipped away to the mountainside to pray. He talked with God and God talked with Him. When others forsook Him, He could always steal away to this tender healing fellowship with God. But now there was no one to whom He could turn— even God had forsaken Him.

When a man goes from a brightly lighted room into the night, he finds the darkness more depressing than if he had gone from a room dimly lighted. So when Jesus, who had basked in the light of God's presence for all eternity, was forced to step out into the blackness of Godforsakenness, it was the hardest thing He had ever endured. No wonder He cried out, "My God, my God, why hast thou forsaken me?"

Does a loving God ever forsake anyone? David said, "God is our refuge." Time after time in the Bible we read these words, "I will never leave thee nor forsake thee." When Israel was in bondage in Egypt God did not forsake her, but He heard her cry and delivered her. When she stood helpless before the Red Sea He did not forsake her. When Daniel was in the lions' den, God did not forsake him. When the Hebrew children were in the fiery furnace, God did not forsake them. In his old age David said, "I have never seen the righteous forsaken." Yet as He hung upon the Cross, Jesus was actually forsaken of God. Had God changed His nature, He who promised never to forsake anyone? Was He angry with His Son? Oh, we cannot understand all the meaning of this amazing cry, but as we follow the Bible truth we can partially comprehend all the sorrow and love and tragedy wrapped up in these words, "My God, my God, why hast thou forsaken me?"

II. WHY WAS JESUS FORSAKEN OF GOD?

Let us look at *Habakkuk 1:13*—"Thou art of purer eyes than to behold evil, and canst not look upon iniquity." We understand here that God's pure eyes cannot look upon sin. Now look at *Isaiah 53:6*—"All we like sheep have gone astray; we have turned everyone to his own way; and the Lord hath laid on Him the iniquity of us all." We see here in the prophecy of the crucifixion that all of our sin was to be laid upon Jesus.

This is not all—listen to *II Corinthians 5:21*—"For He hath made Him to be sin, who knew no sin." We are told here that Christ not only had our sins laid on Him, but that He was made sin for us. Now since a Holy God cannot look upon sin, in these few hours He turned His back upon His Son, who was carrying all our sin in His own body on the tree.

God is so holy, so pure, so free from sin, so full of righteousness that no man can describe Him. He is so holy that even the seraphim in heaven veil their faces before Him. He is so holy that no flesh can stand in His sight one moment. He is so holy that when Isaiah had a vision of His glory, he cried out, "Woe is me, I am undone, for mine eyes hath seen the king, the Lord of Hosts." He is so holy that Job, the best man of his day, when He came into God's presence, said, "I abhor myself." Peter felt the same way when he said to Jesus, "Depart from me, Lord, I am a sinful man." So, of course, though I am sure it broke His own divine heart, when Jesus hung upon that Cross and when all your sins and mine were heaped upon Him, God had to turn His back upon Him.

God is not only holy—He is just. He has some unchangeable laws. If men break these laws a just God must mete out justice. You and I would not think much of a Judge who let favoritism or a bribe influence him to set justice aside. I tell you, God won't do it either. When we sin and break His laws, He says; "I cannot let that pass by. The wages of sin is death—the soul that sinneth, it shall die. Someone must pay the penalty of a broken law." Well, Jesus said, "I will pay the penalty. I will go to the Cross. I will satisfy the law. I will suffer in man's place." When He hung upon the Cross, he paid the last farthing. But as He bore our sins and became separated from God, He cried out, "My God, my God, why hast thou forsaken me?"

When He asked this question no one around the Cross could answer it. The disciples could not answer it. The angels could not. But back in *Psalm 22* we find the answer. This psalm begins with the same words, "My God, my God, why hast thou forsaken me?" It is followed by other cries of loneliness in the same vein. Then in verse 3 of the psalm, we find the answer. "But thou art holy." Jesus in quoting this psalm is simply saying, "I understand, Father. Since thou art holy and since I am full of sin—not mine, but the sin of others—thou must give me this stroke of divine wrath."

Yes, on the Cross Jesus bore all our sins. Think of all the sins of the world gathered together in one heap. Take all the murder and all the adultery and all the dishonesty and all the covetousness and all the idolatry and all the jealousy and all the wrath and all the strife and all the envying and all the back-biting— yes, take all the sin of the world and put it all on Christ, who had no spot or blemish, and you will know what happened at Calvary. But remember this—the sin was not His. It was our seething mass of corruption which was laid upon Him. No wonder He was for-saken. Yet He did not have to bear our sins—He did it because He loved us.

Sin separates from God. Adam and Eve had blessed fellowship with God, but when sin came they hid themselves from Him. The fellowship was broken up— they were separated from God. You and I sometimes walk along in sweet communion with God. Then sin comes into our lives and immediately there is a cloud between us and God. We are still children of God, but sin has separated us from Him. On the Cross Jesus was still God's Son, but sin had separated Him from the Father. Am I addressing someone who once knew the sweetness of God's smile, who walked and talked with the King, who ate at the King's table, but who has allowed sin to come between him and God?

Let me tell you that sin separates from God—it even separated Jesus from Him. I beg you to come back to God, repent of your sin and confess it to Him. Come and let Him restore unto you the joy of His salvation. What was God doing as Jesus hung upon the tree? He was punishing sin. When this old world was sunk in sin and God overflowed the earth with water, He was punishing sin. When He rained hail and brimstone on Sodom and Gomorrah, He was punishing sin. When He sent the plagues upon Egypt and destroyed her armies at the Red Sea, He was punishing sin. How much more was He punishing sin when He forsook Christ and let Him die upon the Cross. All the thunderbolts of Divine Judgment were let loose upon His only Son. He hung there and took it all for you and me. He suffered as much on the Cross as all men could ever suffer through an endless eternity in hell. In that compressed period on the Cross, Jesus suffered the everlasting punishment for the guilt of all sinners. Oh, what suffering! Oh, what a Saviour!

In the Garden of Gethsemane Jesus prayed, "Let this cup pass from me." Now we know what He was talking about. What was in that cup? Not merely a cruel death on the Cross—not merely desertion by His disciples—not merely the denial by His closest friend—not merely the beatings and the stripes and the nails—He could take all of that. No, deep down in that cup He saw this separation from God. He saw God turning His back upon Him and this was the bitterest draught of all.

This separation from God climaxed His sufferings. His own people cried for His blood. The soldiers had mocked Him, they scourged Him with the cruel cato'nine-tails. They buffeted Him and spat in His face, they pierced His hands and feet, they lifted Him up on a Cross. But in spite of all that He suffered at the hands of men, He did not say one word. Now, when the wrath of Heaven falls upon Him, upon our Sin-bearer, it is more than He can stand and He cries out, "My God, my God, why hast thou forsaken me?"

We are told that in the Garden He "sweat as it were great drops of blood." I don't believe this was something that looked like blood, but that His inner anguish actually caused blood to burst out upon His forehead. The deepest cause for this anguish was that He knew He was facing separation from God. The word "Gethsemane" means an "olive press." It was the place where the life-blood of the olives was squeezed out drop by drop. It was well named—for it was there that the Blood of Christ was squeezed out as He faced this awful spiritual suffering.

Why did darkness fall upon the earth? God is Light and the Light is turning away. It is always dark when God turns away. When He turned away the Saviour was left there alone with the sinner's sin—so that the sinner would never be cast into outer darkness, but could live forever in the light of God.

So here is the reason that Jesus was forsaken. You and I have sinned. He bore our sins on the cross. God could not look upon that sin, so He forsook His Son. There Christ was forsaken of God that we might never be forsaken. Thank God, because of what He did, you and I will never be condemned to eternal suffering if we put our trust in Him.

Romans 8:1—"There is therefore now no condemnation to them which are in Christ Jesus, who walk not after the flesh, but after the spirit."

III. LET US LOOK AT SOME LESSONS FOR OUR
OWN HEARTS

1. *In spite of all His sufferings, Jesus never wavered in His faith.* He still called God, "My God." He had said on many occasions that God was always with Him, but now God has withdrawn from Him, He has turned His back upon Him. Does Jesus therefore doubt God? Does He say, "I was mistaken"? Does He give up? No—He holds on to His implicit faith in God.

All visible support was gone, even God was not there. There was no hope of deliverance. He must see this thing through. But even then He took refuge in His faith. He could say with one of his later followers, "I know that all things work together for good to them that love God." Job said, "Though He slay me, yet will I trust Him." Jesus was now being slain and God was allowing it. Yet Jesus still trusted Him.

It is easy to trust God and sing when the sun is shining, but what about the testing time, when the sun fades out of the sky? A Christian should have a faith which helps in adversity as well as prosperity. I have seen some people who talked glibly about their faith in God, but in the time of sorrow they cried out in despair, like others who had no hope. The real Christian has a faith to live by and a faith to die by. His faith stood the test. Will yours?

2. *Our salvation was wrought out as He cried, "My God, my God, why hast thou forsaken Me?"* On the Cross all of our sins were laid on Him. Divine judgment fell upon His shoulders. Not only did He take our sins, but He suffered the penalty for them. Now we can go free when by faith we appropriate all He did on the Cross for us. Down in Egypt a lamb was slain—a lamb without spot or blemish. The lamb's blood was then placed on the door-post and lintels of

the door. Then God said, "When I see the blood I will pass over you." On Calvary a Man died, God died. He poured out a blood offering, He satisfied the law's demands. The minute you and I come to Him and trust Him as our Saviour, God says, "I see the blood. I don't see your sins. I will save you and keep you saved forever."

3. *Here is the greatest love in heaven and earth.* Jesus abhorred sin, He loathed sin, His holy soul shrank from it. But on the Cross all our sins were laid upon Him and sin coiled itself about Him like a poisonous serpent. And He willingly endured it all. Why? Because He loved us.

John 15:13—"Greater love hath no man than this, that a man lay down his life for his friends."

John 13:1—"Now before the feast of the passover, when Jesus knew that His hour was come that He should depart out of this world unto the Father, having loved His own which were in the world, He loved them unto the end."

Is there anyone in this world who would drink a cup of poison to save you? Jesus did. Is there anyone who would take a rattlesnake into his bosom to save you? Jesus did. Is there anyone in the prime of life who would turn his back upon everything and die to save you? Jesus did. Some day we will see Him in glory. We will see the prints of the nails in His hands and feet. We will hear again the old, old story of what He did for us on Calvary. When at last we fully realize what it all meant to Him—when we understand what He saved us from and what He saved us to, surely we will cry out, "It was all for me—for me." All through the endless ages we will never cease to thank Him.

4. *Here is a warning to the unsaved.* God is merci-

ful. He proved this when He provided a Saviour. He proves it when He invites us to come unto Him. He proves it by His long-suffering. But there is a limit to His mercy. Some day the door of hope will be closed. Death may come suddenly and "after death the judgment." In that day He will deal in justice and not in mercy. If you have refused and rejected Christ, there will be no mercy for you. If you trample Him under foot, you seal your own doom.

The gospel call today is one of mercy. Christ pleads for you to accept Him and be saved. His favorite word is "Come." He says, "Come unto Me, ye thieves, ye harlots, ye blasphemers, ye murderers, ye good moral men. Come unto Me, all ye sinners, and I will save you." It will not be so in the Day of Judgment. There will be no mercy then. There will be no sermons, no invitations, no further chance. If you go through life turning down every opportunity, if you come to the end of the way without Christ, out there in eternity you will cry out, "Have mercy upon me." But the door of mercy will be closed and the angels will cry out, "Time's up." Because you will not answer His call here, you will be lost out there forever.

Jesus suffered greatly on the Cross. All that He endured you must endure in hell if you reject Him as your Saviour. You will be separated from every good thing. You will be forsaken of God. You will go down to be tormented forever and ever in the lake of fire. No love there, no light there, no hope there. There is nothing good there, because God is not there.

God spared not the Lord Jesus when He found sin on Him—the sin of others. Do you think He will spare you if you come up to judgment with your own sin on you? If He poured out His wrath on Him who bore no sin but ours, do you think He will hold back

His wrath if you go on in sin and come to the end of the way with your sin still on you? But there is hope for you. "He that believeth on the Son hath life, but he that believeth not the Son shall not see life, but the wrath of God abideth on him."

Admiral Chen of the Chinese Navy sat with some friends in an evangelistic service in Canton. He was deeply moved by the sermon. The preacher made an appeal and decision cards were passed out. The Admiral took out his pencil. He was going to sign the card which said, "I accept Christ as my personal Saviour." One of his companions said, "Don't be in a hurry to do that—take some time to think it over." The Admiral put his pencil back into his pocket. At the end of the service he and his friend walked out of the building. A soldier, who had been waiting outside, stepped up and shot the Admiral, killing him instantly. For him there was no further chance.

I beg you to make your decision tonight. You may not have another chance. "Prepare to meet thy God."

5

"CHRIST'S CRY OF HUMAN SUFFERING"

After this, Jesus knowing that all things were now accomplished, that the Scripture might be fulfilled, saith, I thirst (John 19:28).

Tonight we come again to Calvary. CALVARY—where we come with our sin and receive a Saviour's righteousness. CALVARY—where we come with our ruin and receive His perfection. CALVARY—where we come with our bitterness and receive His sweetness. CALVARY—where we come with our despair and receive His assurance. CALVARY—where we come with our darkness and receive His light. CALVARY—where we come with our sorrow and receive His joy. CALVARY—where we come with our hell and receive His heaven.

In these sermons we have been watching Jesus die on the Cross. We have heard Him pray for His persecutors; we have heard Him promise Paradise to a penitent thief; we have heard Him make provision for His mother; we have heard Him cry out unto God in the darkness of God-forsakenness. Tonight as we come again to the Cross, we see that He cannot live much longer. The darkness now is gone and the sun is shining again. Now we hear His cry, "I thirst." The soldiers had a vessel of vinegar nearby and one of them dipped a sponge in this vinegar and pressed it to His lips.

Now even this small detail had been prophesied. Every detail of the crucifixion had been written down beforehand in the Bible. Listen to *Psalm 69:21*—"They gave me also gall for my meat; and in my thirst they gave me vinegar to drink."

This is one reason why we know that the Bible is the inerrant Word of God. It predicts a thing in detail, a thing no human being ever dreamed of, and hundreds of years later this thing happens just as it was predicted.

> How firm a foundation, ye saints of the Lord,
> Is laid for your faith in His excellent Word.

Now let us "pitch our mental tents" around this cry from the Cross and seek to learn some great lessons for our hearts.

I. WE SEE HERE HOW GREATLY JESUS SUFFERED

It has been said that death by crucifixion is the most painful mode of torture ever conceived by man. The draining away of the blood brings on intensive thirst. Hunger is painful, but it is nothing compared to the pangs of thirst. No wonder Jesus cried out, "I thirst." Let us look at what preceded this cry and we will understand something of His physical suffering. Just the night before He instituted the Lord's Supper in the Upper Room; then He spoke for sometime to the disciples; then He went into the Garden of Gethsemane. There He passed through an hour of great agony. His soul was exceeding sorrowful unto death. He was in such anguish that He sweat drops of blood. When He came out of the Garden, Judas, the traitor, kissed Him and the mob rushed up to arrest Him. In the middle of the night He was taken before Caiaphas, where he was examined and condemned. He was held there until the morning without rest; then He was taken before Pilate where He went through a lengthy trial. After that He was taken before Herod, where He was mocked and ridiculed. Then He was taken back to Pilate. Pilate commanded Him to be scourged, the crown of thorns was pressed down upon His brow, and the soldiers mocked Him, saying, "Hail, King of the Jews!"

After another delay He was sentenced to death, the heavy cross was placed upon His bleeding back and the journey to Calvary was begun. Weak from all that He had endured, He fainted beneath the load, and another man was called upon to carry His cross. Soon they reached the top of Calvary, His hands and feet were nailed to the Cross, and He was lifted up upon the tree. He hung there for three hours in the noonday heat, then for three hours of darkness. Yet He never murmured, He never complained. He bore His sufferings in majestic silence. Now His whole body is racked with pain, His mouth is parched, His throat is burning. No wonder He cries out, "I thirst."

Not only did He suffer in body, but in spirit. He had just emerged from three hours of darkness. During that time, God had forsaken Him and turned His back upon Him. This spiritual conflict added greatly to His suffering. He had been for a time in a land where God was not—no wonder a terrible drouth filled His body and spirit. Let us go back to Psalm 42:3—"My soul thirsteth for God, for the living God." So we see here that His thirst was not only physical, but spiritual. He had been cut off from fellowship with God, and now His soul thirsts for the sweet communion which He had enjoyed with the Father for all eternity past.

I have already told you that Jesus suffered on the Cross as much as a sinner could ever suffer in an eternity of hell. He suffered so much that He cried out, "I thirst." How much more then will be your eternal suffering in hell if you go through life rejecting Him!

You will go down into the lake of fire and suffer forever even as Jesus suffered on the Cross.

II. HERE WE SEE THE HUMAN SIDE OF CHRIST

There were two sides to Christ's nature—divine and human. He was all of God and all of man. He was truly the God-Man. There has never been another like Him. Man is all of man and none of God. God is all of God and none of man. But Jesus was both. In Him divinity and humanity were perfectly blended.

On the Divine side He lived in heaven with God. He created the heavens and the earth. He made man and put him in the world. He ruled over the angels, guided the destinies of men and nations, and had all power in heaven and earth. On the human side He came down into the world, He was born of a human mother, He lived an earthly life, He talked and laughed and wept and had all the normal human impulses.

As God He walked upon the waters, He stilled the stormy seas, He cast out devils, He healed the sick and raised the dead. As a man He hungered and thirsted and suffered pain. He was tempted in all points like as we are, and He felt all the emotions of men. On the human side He was a servant—on the divine side He was a King. On the human side He wept at the grave of Lazarus—on the Divine side He called Lazarus back unto life again. He was just as human as we are, with only one difference. But, oh, what a difference! He was a perfect human. Sin could never get inside His heart and Satan could never control one inch of Him.

Now even on the Cross we see these two sides. On the Divine side He promised to take the dying thief home to heaven—and He had the power to do it. On the human side He suffered such great agony that He cried out, "I thirst." Here is evidence of His perfect humanity—the fact that He thirsted. God does not thirst, the angels do not thirst, we will not thirst in heaven. *Revelation 7:16*—"They shall hunger no more, neither thirst any more." We thirst now because we are human, living in a world of sorrow. Christ thirsted on the Cross because He was human, suffering and dying for our sins.

Why did Jesus become human? Why did He take upon Himself the form of man? Why didn't God send Him down full-grown into the world, and then let Him die for our sins? Why did He bring Him through the womb of Mary and the stable of Bethlehem and the carpenter shop of Nazareth? Surely He came this way that He might go through all the trials and difficulties of a human life, so that He could understand us and sympathize with us in all our trials and difficulties.

Who can help me most in my sorrow? Surely it is the one who has been through the same sorrow. Well, nothing will ever happen to you in the way of sorrow which did not happen to Jesus. He is the One that we want when we need help and sympathy. The One who cried, "I thirst" knows what suffering is and He can help me when I suffer. Thank God, He knows all about us. He does care. He is touched with our grief, He knows when the sad heart aches till it nearly breaks. He knows when we have said good-bye to the dearest on earth to us. He knows, He cares, He sympathizes, He comforts. No matter how deep down into despair you have gone—no matter how rough the pathway— no matter how heavy the heart, Jesus invites you to come and bring it all to Him. I Peter 5:7—"Casting all your care upon Him, for He careth for you."

Is your body racked with pain? So was His. Are you misunderstood and misrepresented? So was He.

Have those who are nearest and dearest turned away from you? They did from Him. Are you in the darkness? He was for three hours. He ran the gamut of all the sufferings and the trials of all men, climaxed by His death on the Cross, and His awful cry of anguish, "I thirst." So when we suffer, we can go to Him and say, "Lord, thou hast suffered more than any man. I am going down in the sea of woe. Help me." I tell you that He will then reach down from the Cross, throw His arms around you and give you the peace that passeth all understanding. Yes, the One who suffered most knows how to sympathize with us when we suffer.

Dr. George W. Truett told this story of two young mothers. The baby of the first mother died, and Dr. Truett conducted the funeral. She and her husband were not Christians; they were worldly and Godless, and he had a difficult time reaching them. He invited them to his church and to Christ. They came to the services and a few Sunday nights later, they were both saved. They became faithful Christians and God's comfort was theirs. Then one day he was called to another funeral. The second mother had lost her little baby girl. This mother was not a Christian and she was utterly broken and desolate. The preacher read the sweetest Scriptures; he prayed earnestly; he said the tenderest words and the quartette sang their most comforting songs. But none of these things seemed to reach the broken-hearted mother. Then the first young mother, who now knew Christ, slipped over to her side. She whispered, "Jennie, everything is going to be all right." "Mary, it can't be, everything is dark and wrong." "But I passed through all of this, God called me and through the darkness I came to Him. He comforted me, and He will comfort you. Just put your trust in Christ and cling to Him and He will bring you through." The preacher said that this mother did more to help and comfort the other mother than he could have done in months.

Yes, the one who has suffered can sympathize with us when we suffer. If a human being can help us in an hour like this, how much more can Jesus, who knows what the depths of suffering are.

III. WE HEAR NOW THE CRY OF THE VICTOR

On the Cross Jesus fought out His battle with Satan. He won the victory and secured salvation for all men. Now He stands aside, as it were, to look for a moment at the completed task. When He saw that He had done all He could for lost men, when He saw that He had won the battle for them, then He thought of His own famished and thirsty body, and He cried out, "I thirst." Yes, it was the cry of a victor.

A racer gives his best to the race. He strains every nerve, never thinking of his own need. He just wants to win the race. When he breaks the tape as the victor, when the crowd applauds his victory, then he realizes his own need and he asks for a drink of water. So Jesus hung six hours on the Cross. He gave all that He had, He fought the fiercest battle, He endured the deepest agony. Now with the victory won, He thinks of His own need and cries, "I thirst." Yes, He thirsted there so that we need never know the awful thirst and the bitter anguish that He knew as He died for us. "Hallelujah, what a Saviour!"

IV. WE SEE ONE HERE WHO CAN SATISFY OUR THIRST

Man is a thirsty creature—he is always seeking to satisfy that thirst. One man is thirsty for wealth and will do anything to get it. One man is thirsty for honors and high position, and will give up all of his convictions and make every compromise to reach the top. This is the reason that most great men are not great Christians. They make so many deals, they stifle their consciences so many times on the way up that they lose all their spiritual strength. One man is thirsty for the things of the flesh and he breaks holy vows and commits the scarlet sin. One man is thirsty for pleasure and he drinks at every fountain of worldliness. One man is thirsty for knowledge and he searches high and low to gain it. Yes, men go through life thirsting for something.

These things do not bring permanent satisfaction and joy. Jesus said, "Whosoever drinketh of this water shall thirst again." It is true. You can try all the fountains of the world—they satisfy but for a moment and soon the zest is gone. God made us so that these things can never satisfy our souls. Solomon tried everything under the sun and then cried out, "All is vanity and vexation of Spirit." We have many church members today who are not satisfied. They go out and give their time and energy to worldly institutions and organizations, and yet they do not receive the satisfaction that Jesus would give them if they lived close to Him and followed Him every day.

Why will not these worldly things satisfy? Because the thirst of the soul is a spiritual thirst and only Christ can satisfy that thirst. He said, "Whosoever drinketh of the water that I shall give him, shall never thirst."

Oh, soul, He is the only One who can meet your deep needs; He alone can quench your thirst; He alone can give you peace. He made the water to gush forth in the wilderness for the children of Israel, He turned the water into wine, He can quench your thirst. It is not a creed nor a form that you need, but a Person, the Lord Jesus Christ. He stands with His arms wide open saying, "Come unto me all ye that labor and are heavy laden and I will give you rest."

Yes, Jesus fully satisfies. When I think of all that He has done for me, I say, "He satisfies." When I think of the joy that He gives me as I walk by His side, I say, "He satisfies." In all eternity, as I enjoy the bliss of heaven and as I look upon His face, I will sing, "I am satisfied with Jesus."

Jesus thirsted on the Cross and He still thirsts. Backslider, He thirsts for you. Once you walked with Him, and worked for Him, but now you have backslidden into the ways of the world. He wants you to come back. He longs to have fellowship with you. Just think of it—you can offer Christ something which satisfies His heart. You lost something when you forsook Christ. You lost the joy of your salvation, and you lost your spiritual influence and power. Not only that, but you cheated Jesus of your fellowship and service. So He says to you tonight, "I have been missing you. I am thirsty for your fellowship. Come back and walk by My side and help Me in My Work." Can you deny that plea?

He thirsts for lost souls, also. One day He stopped by a well. He was hungry and thirsty. He had sent His disciples into the town to buy food, and He desired water from the well. But when the disciples came back, He told them that He did not want any food and so far as we know He never drank of the water of that well. What had happened to satisfy Him? A woman had come to the well, a great sinner, and He had won her to faith and salvation. That satisfied Him more than food and drink. He thirsts for you even now. You can make your own heart glad and you can satisfy His thirst if you will only come to Him.

There are some hearing or reading these words without Christ. If you die in your sins, throughout eternity you will cry, "I thirst." In the lake of fire you will suffer forever amid the flames. If Christ suffered such awful thirst when He felt God's wrath for three hours, what will your suffering be? Millions of years will go by and you will still be thirsting with no hope of relief. Ten million years will go by and you will still be suffering. The rich man in hell cried out to Abraham in heaven, "I am tormented in this flame." Will this be your cry?

There is hope for everyone! Turn your back upon sin and unbelief and come to the waiting arms of Jesus. He will put His love around you and forgive you and save you and take you home to Glory, for He says, "Him that cometh to me, I will in no wise cast out."

One Sunday afternoon Billy Sunday preached in a great tabernacle in Atlanta. At the close of the service he gave an invitation. I walked down the aisle and gave my heart to Christ. Today I thank God for that decision. Because of it life has been sweeter and richer and more satisfying. Because of it I have hope for the life to come. Listen, what Jesus has done for others He can do for you. Leave your sins, confess Him, put all your trust in Him, and He will give you the water of life which will satisfy your thirst forever.

6

"CHRIST'S CRY OF TRIUMPH"

> When Jesus therefore had received the vinegar, he said, It is finished; and he bowed his head and gave up the ghost (John 19:30).

Tonight we come again to Calvary. CALVARY—where God so loved the world that He gave His only begotten Son. CALVARY—where God commended His love toward us. CALVARY—where Christ Himself bore our sins in His own body. CALVARY—where He was wounded for our transgressions, bruised for our iniquities, where the chastisement of our peace was upon Him, and where by His stripes we are healed. CALVARY—where echoes the cry, "Believe on the Lord Jesus Christ and thou shalt be saved!"

In the last two messages we heard Jesus' cry from the Cross: "My God, my God, why hast thou forsaken me?" and "I thirst." These words portrayed His sorrow and suffering, both physical and spiritual. Now we hear a different cry. It is a cry of triumph, of victory, of jubilation. Jesus cries out, "It is finished." The victim has become the victor. The Saviour's sufferings are over. His work on earth is done and the gates of heaven are now opened up, so that any man may enter in who puts his faith in this faithful Saviour.

There are three words here in the English, but in the language which Jesus spoke there is only one. In that

word is wrapped up the whole Gospel of Christ. In
that one word we find the entire basis for our salvation. In that one word we find the ground for all of
our assurance. In that one word we find all of our
hope of eternal life. Yes, when Jesus said, "It is
finished," He meant that He had done everything necessary to save and bless you and me for time and
Eternity.

In a few minutes He is going to die. The awful cup
has been drained to the last bitter dregs; the dreadful
darkness is over; the precious blood has been shed;
the outpoured wrath of God for sin has been endured.
All that remains now is the act of death. That is a
small thing for Him, for in His mind and heart this has
already been accomplished. So now He cries, "It is
finished." What did Jesus mean when He said this?

I. He Meant That All the Prophecies Connected
   with His Life and Death Had Been Fulfilled

A most interesting Bible study is to read the prophecy
of the Old Testament, and then come to the New Testament and see this prophecy literally fulfilled. The Bible
is true itself because God is true. If He predicts a thing,
you can know that it will come to pass. Hundreds of
years before Christ was born, prophecy declared that
He would be born of a woman, that His mother would
be a virgin, that He would be a descendant of David,
that He would be named before He was born, that He
would be born in Bethlehem, that He would flee to
Egypt, that He would be poor and needy, that He would
have a forerunner, John the Baptist, that He would
cause the lame to walk, the deaf to hear, and the dumb
to speak. All of this has now happened.

It was prophesied that He would be despised and
rejected of men, that He would be hated without a

cause, that He would be betrayed by friends, that He would be forsaken by His disciples, that He would be led to the slaughter, that He would be numbered among the transgressors, and that the soldiers would gamble for His garments. Now when He cries, "It is finished," we know that all of this has come to pass.

There are two lines of prophecy in the Old Testament relating to Christ. The first line had to do with His first coming, and all of these prophecies have been literally fulfilled. The second line has to do with His Second Coming. As we have seen the first line of prophecy fulfilled, so can we know that the second line will be fulfilled, also. He came the first time to earth in humiliation—He is coming back the second time in glory. The Bible says so, and no man has a right to say that these things will not happen.

Down through the years Israel had looked for the coming Messiah. They talked about Him, sang about Him, and they dreamed about Him. When He did not come, it seems that their hope grew dim. Their prophecies became mixed up with tradition and when the Messiah did come, they had the wrong idea about Him. They looked for a King instead of a Suffering Servant, and therefore they did not recognize Him. "He came to His own and His own received Him not." When He was here, He said that He was coming back again. The years have gone by and He has not returned. Men have said, "Where is the promise of His coming? For since the fathers fell asleep, all things continue as they were from the beginning" (II Peter 3:4).

Today men mix the prophecy of the Bible with the modernism of this day and say that only symbolic language was used in the prophecies, and Jesus is not coming back. Thus they throw part of the Bible away and rob themselves and others of the Blessed Hope. But

I tell you, as He came the first time, so shall He come again. He will come first in the air to take up His redeemed people, then He will come to earth to set up His Kingdom and rule with the saints in that Kingdom. As we look back to the Cross and hear Jesus cry, "It is finished," we know that He meant that the Scriptures had been fulfilled. So shall all the prophecies concerning His second Coming be fulfilled, also.

II. HE MEANT THAT HIS SUFFERINGS WERE OVER

He was called, "The Man of Sorrows." No man ever had a more fitting title. He suffered at the hands of, men, of Satan and of God. God bruised Him and forsook Him on the Cross because there He bore our sins. His friends and His enemies inflicted pain upon Him. It was not just on the Cross that He suffered—He suffered all through His life.

Someone has painted a picture of Jesus as a boy in the carpenter's shop of Nazareth. He stands before a window and holds his arms out toward either side of the window. The rays of the sun reflect His shadow upon the wall, and behold, it is the shadow of a cross. He lived in the shadow of that Cross all of his life, knowing that one day He would hang there for the sins of all men, forsaken of God and man. Everywhere that He went, there was the shadow of the Cross looming up before Him. He went to a wedding in Cana, where all was gladness and laughter, and the shadow was there. We hear Him saying, "My time has not yet come." Nicodemus came to see Him at night and Jesus talked to him about how the Son of Man would be lifted up; and there was the shadow. James and John came and asked Him to give them high places of honor in His Kingdom, and He had to talk to them of the cup of suffering and the bap-

tism of sorrow. There was the shadow. Peter con-
fessed that he was "Christ, the Son of the Living
God." Jesus had to tell them, then, that He must
go up to Jerusalem and be killed. There was the
shadow. On the Mount of Transfiguration, when
Moses and Elijah came down, what did they talk
about? They talked about His death. There was the
shadow that never left Him.

Can you imagine how you would feel if you knew absolutely that one day you would die a violent death and
suffer as He did? You would think of it as you rose
up in the morning, as you sat down to your meals,
as you went to work, as you went out to enjoy fellowship with your friends, as you lay down to sleep at
night. Surely, such a thing would run you stark, raving
mad. You could not stand it. Yet, it was that way
with Jesus.

Still, if Jesus suffered under the shadow of a cross,
think how much more He suffered from the real thing.
In the prime of His young manhood His hour comes.
He goes into Gethsemane and fights out His battle.
Drained of strength and blood, He comes out saying,
"Not my will, but Thine be done." He appears four
times at unjust trials. They scourge Him and buffet Him
and spit upon Him and crown Him with thorns. Soon
He is on the way to the Cross, soon He is nailed to the
tree, soon He is raised up between heaven and earth.
From earth the people jeered and taunted Him—from
heaven darkness descended and God turned His back
upon Him. Well might He cry out in the words of
Lamentations 1:12—"Is it nothing to you, all ye that
pass by? Behold, and see if there be any sorrow like
unto my sorrow, which is done unto me, wherewith the
Lord hath afflicted me in the day of His fierce anger."

Now the suffering is over, both physical and spiritual.

The cup has been drained, the storm of God's wrath is spent, the darkness is ended, the wages of sin have been paid and the law has been satisfied. All the shame and suffering and agony are past. Never again will Jesus experience pain. Never again will He be reviled and cruelly treated by human hands. Never again will God turn His back upon Him. All His sufferings are over. And as we think of all the agony and suffering of the Cross, it ought to cause us to love Him more as we remember it was all for us.

III. HE MEANT THAT HIS WORK OF REDEMPTION WAS ACCOMPLISHED

There are three persons in the God-head and each of them has a definite task. God the Father is especially concerned with the government of the world. He rules all the works of His hands. God the Son is especially interested in the work of redemption. He came into the world to die for sinners. God the Holy Spirit is especially interested in the Scriptures. He moved men to write the Bible and He interprets it to our hearts.

Now on the Cross Christ has finished His work. God created the heavens and the earth and all that is in them, and He could say, "It is finished." Christ died upon the Cross only after He had completely finished His work. No one will ever have to add anything to it in order to save a soul. He looked upon the work that He had done, and He said, "It stands finished, it is complete, it is done." It was a word of accomplishment, a word of victory. Isaiah 53:6—"All we like sheep have gone astray, we have turned everyone to His own way; and the Lord hath laid on him the iniquity of us all." Now it is done—He has borne our sins and our redemption is complete. In Revelation

5:9 we hear the song of heaven. "Thou wast slain, and hast redeemed us to God by thy blood out of every kindred and tongue and people and nation."

It is all done now. He has done it all. Redemption is complete and anyone in the wide world can be saved. Jesus says, "Look unto me, all ye ends of the earth, and be ye saved." Let the rich man look and let the poor man look. Let the great and the small look. Let the high and the low look. Let the ignorant and the educated look. Let the deep-dyed sinner and the good moral man look. All of them need to be saved, and He has done enough to save them all. They need simply to look to Him in saving faith and they will surely be saved.

Jesus came from heaven's glory to earth's shame for this purpose. He laid aside the robes of royalty and took upon Himself the garments of our sinful humanity for this purpose. He was born in Bethlehem for this purpose; He entered the ministry for this purpose; He walked among sinners for this purpose; He sweat blood in Gethsemane for this purpose; He wore the crown of thorns for this purpose; He died on Calvary for this purpose. Now this purpose is accomplished, the Divinely-given task is performed. He has done something which the angels in heaven could not do. He has wrought our redemption. Nothing remains to be added; He has done enough to save every sinner on earth.

Christ came to "seek and save that which was lost." Now the lost ones can be saved because He took their place and bore their sins. He came to "redeem them that were under the law." The redemption price now has been fully paid. He came to "take away our sins." Now He has taken them away through the shedding of His precious blood. It is all done now—it is finished.

Today men think that salvation is a matter of their

own works. They want to do something in order to be saved. No, it is a matter of Christ's work. He has already done it all.

An English evangelist had just closed the last service of a revival and was busy taking down his tent. A young man came to him and said: "Sir, what must I do to be saved?" The evangelist replied, "You are too late, my friend, too late." "You don't mean that I am too late just because your meeting is closed, do you?" Then the evangelist said, "Young man, you want to do something to be saved. I tell you that you are too late by hundreds of years. The work of salvation was completed upon the Cross. Jesus said so. Now nothing that you can do will save you. You must simply fall upon your knees and accept the Saviour and what He has already done for you." The young man saw the light, trusted Christ, and was saved.

Suppose that you owed $1,000.00 at the bank and could not pay a penny of it. Suppose then that I went to the bank and paid it for you and brought you the cancelled note. What would you have to do to get clear of the debt? Absolutely nothing—all that you would need to do would be to accept what I had done for you. Well, you have sinned. There is a great debt in heaven against you, a debt which you cannot pay. But Christ on the Cross put His blood up there as payment, blood precious enough and valuable enough to pay for all the sins of your lifetime. Now what must you do to get the debt cancelled? Nothing that you can do will cancel the debt. Everything has already been done and all that you have to do is to appropriate by faith what Christ did for you upon the Cross.

> But drops of grief can ne'er repay
> The debt of love I owe,
> Here, Lord, I give myself away,
> 'Tis all that I can do.

Adam and Eve, after they had sinned, sought a covering for their sins. They used leaves for this covering. God saw that this was an ineffective covering, so He killed some animals and used their skins to cover Adam and Eve. Now in His death Christ had provided an everlasting and sufficient covering for sin. In Noah's time the flood came and God saved eight people in the Ark. Now Christ has built an Ark of Safety for all who want to be saved. Down in Egypt, when the blood was put upon the doorpost on that fateful night, the death angel saw the blood and passed over that home. Now the Lamb of God has spilt His blood. Get your soul under that blood and you will be safe forever. In the wilderness the serpents bit the Israelites, and they were dying like flies. Moses told them to look to the brazen serpent and they would be cured. Jesus said, "Even as Moses lifted up the serpent in the wilderness, even so must the son of man be lifted up, that whosoever believeth in him should not perish, but have eternal life." He has been lifted up now and all who look to Him are cured of Satan's sin-bite. It is all finished.

Dr. Russell Bradley Jones tells us that three realms were interested in this cry, "It is finished." First, heaven was interested. At the end of the World War, when the news came back that the fighting was over, the people of our nation greatly rejoiced. Some of them danced in the streets, some prayed and gave thanks in the churches; some knelt in silence in their homes and praised God. Now as Jesus finishes the work which God gave Him to do the news is flashed to heaven. It was then that the angels sang their sweetest songs, for the war was now over, the victory was won, and the Son of God would soon be coming home. God could not bring lost men to heaven until the price of redemption had been paid. Now this price is paid and without violating His holy justice, God can receive lost men who come through the merits and the finished work of Jesus Christ.

Someone has said that the Old Testament saints, Abraham, Isaac, Jacob, Moses, David and the others got into heaven on credit. They looked forward in faith to the One who would pay the price for their sins, and a home in heaven was given to them upon promise of that payment. The promise has now been fulfilled and the debt has been. paid. Their hearts are full of joy, for Christ has not failed them.

Hell was also interested in this cry. Those in hell are now absolutely helpless. Their doom is sealed, the great gulf is fixed, and they can never get out of the place of punishment. Even Satan knows that he is doomed and that it is just a matter of time before he is cast into the lake of fire. Christ has crushed him.

Earth was also interested in this cry. To some the cry of the Cross brings happiness. They know that their salvation is not dependent upon their poor works, but upon the fine, finished work of Jesus. If we must depend upon our poor selves to get to heaven, we are doomed forever. But, thank God, we can depend upon Jesus and He will never fail us.

There are some who do not understand the full meaning of this cry. They say, "Yes, I know that Jesus did much there upon the Cross, but it is not enough. I will have to do something." So they add baptism, or the Lord's Supper, or their gifts, or their good lives, or their works. They think that salvation is in these things. I tell you that we must not depend upon the works of our hands. We must lean wholly upon Jesus. These things are a matter of obedience which should come after we have been saved.

Some are indifferent to this cry. It matters not to

them that Christ died upon the Cross. They are taken up with pleasure, with lusts of the flesh, with worldly living, with money and stocks and bonds and appetites. They are seeking satisfaction in this world, not knowing that Jesus included that satisfaction in the salvation which He wrought out upon Calvary. Yes, He did everything on the Cross necessary to save us.

On a certain holiday Hudson Taylor was left alone. Time hung heavy on his hands. He began to read a religious tract, since there was nothing else for him to do. As he read the tract, he came upon these words, "The finished work of Christ." These words struck his youthful heart. He wanted to be saved, but thought that he had to appease God by something that he could do himself. Later he said, "There was nothing for me to do but fall upon my knees, accept the Saviour and praise Him forevermore."

That is the only thing for you to do, my friend. "Well," you ask, "shouldn't I do these other things, also? Shouldn't I be baptized and join the church and partake of the Lord's Supper and tithe and serve the Lord?" Yes, you should do all of these things, but they are to come after you have been saved. Come to Him and be saved by His work for you on the Cross. He will fill your heart with peace and you will find great joy in doing these things in His Name. But you will do them, then, not in order *to* be saved, but because you *have* been saved.

A certain man was an infidel—a hard drinker—a man who mistreated his wife. One day when he was sobering up after a drunken spree, he was filled with remorse. He felt that he wanted to die, but he did not have the courage to commit suicide. So he went down to the wharf and lay down on the edge of the boat. He was hoping that he would fall asleep, roll over into the water and drown. He did fall asleep, but when he awakened the stars were shining overhead and he was sober. It was midnight and he decided to go home. As he came up to his house, he saw his wife through the window. She was ironing one of his shirts and in spite of all the poverty and trouble he had brought upon her, she was singing, "What a Friend We Have in Jesus." The man, with a breaking heart, went in and said to his wife, "If Jesus can make my poor wife sing at midnight, He can help me. Tell me how to be saved." Soon he was rejoicing in his salvation and he became a fine Christian.

Listen, Christ died that you might have such a friend and that you might have such a song in your heart. He closed His part of the deal on Calvary when He cried out, "It is finished." You can come now and close your part of the deal by trusting Him as your Saviour. Will you come?

7

"CHRIST'S CRY OF SOUL - COMMITTAL"

> And when Jesus had cried with a loud voice, he said, Father, into thy hands I commend my spirit; and having said thus, He gave up the ghost (Luke 23:46).

Tonight we come again to Calvary. CALVARY—where we hear the sweetest story ever told. CALVARY—where the chasm between God and man was bridged forever. CALVARY—where man climbed out of his sin to the Heavenly Father's security. CALVARY—where God loved as no one has ever loved. CALVARY—where Christ gave all that He had that we might have all of heaven. CALVARY—where Christ finished the redemptive work God sent Him to do. CALVARY—where our poor souls find salvation and satisfaction, happiness and heaven. Oh Calvary, how poor, how helpless, how hopeless we would all be if it were not for thee!

Seven times did Jesus speak from the Cross. This is the number of perfection. Christ was perfection in every way.

(1) He spoke to God in behalf of others—"Father, forgive them."

(2) He spoke to the thief and promised heaven to him—"This day shalt thou be with me in paradise."

(3) He spoke to John and provided for His mother—"Behold, thy mother."

(4) He spoke in a cry to God—"My God, my God, why hast thou forsaken me?"

79

(5) He spoke to the spectators—"I thirst."

(6) He spoke to heaven, earth and hell—"It is finished."

(7) He speaks again to God—"Father, into thy hands I commend my spirit."

Seven is also the number for rest after a finished work. In six days God made the world and all that is in it—on the seventh day He rested. Now Jesus' work of redemption is done—His sixth word was, "It is finished." Now His seventh word brings Him to a place of rest, in His Father's hands.

I. WE SEE HERE A WONDERFUL CHANGE

Six hours He has hung upon the Cross. Three hours He suffered at the hands of Satan and men—three hours He suffered separation from God. Now it is all over and He is back again in communion with the Father. What a wonderful change! It was like going from a hovel to a palace, from darkness to light, from hell to heaven. Up until the time when He hung upon the Cross, He had perfect communion with the father. He prayed during the forty days in the wilderness, He prayed before day, He prayed all night, He prayed before any crisis or great undertaking. He could slip away any time and pray and find Himself in perfect communion with the Father. There was never a cloud between Him and God——no sin ever blocked the way.

The word, "Father," is a beautiful title. He used it over and over. As a boy there were times when I could not face my father. But Jesus could always look up into His Father's face and know that there was "nothing between." But on the Cross a dreadful thing happened. Because He was bearing our sins, He became separated from God. God forsook Him for a time and turned His back upon Him. Now Christ has taken all the guilt for our sins upon Himself, He has paid the full price. He has suffered hell's punishment for us. The work is done, so the cloud lifts, and Jesus is back in the loving arms of His Father, in a fellowship sweeter than ever before.

As long as He was in the hands of men, His plight was a sorrowful one. He knew what was coming, however, and He did not shrink from it. Hear what He says in Matthew 17:22, 23—"The son of man shall be betrayed into the hands of men, and they shall kill him." In Gethsemane, when He found that His disciples had gone to sleep while He was praying, He said sadly, "Sleep on now and take your rest, the Son of man is betrayed into the hands of sinners." He knew that He would be given over to sinful men. Since He had all power in heaven and earth, He could have avoided arrest, He could have struck the mob with sudden death. But the time had come for Him, the time to suffer for our sins and He willingly gave Himself up. And, oh, how these wicked men did take advantage of their opportunity! They gave full vent to their hatred of Him. They did their worst. They inflicted their cruelest torture upon Him, they made Him suffer to the very limit.

Now it is all over. The appointed work is finished. He voluntarily delivers His spirit into the hands of God. Never again can men torture Him, never again will He be at the mercy of wicked sinners, never again will He suffer shame. He commits Himself to God. God will look after Him now. It is a fearful thing for a sinner to fall into the hands of the living God, but it is a wonderful thing for His Only Son to fall into the hands of a loving Father.

What did the Father do for Him? Three days later He raised Him from the dead. Forty days later He took

Him home to heaven. He exalted Him high above all principalities and powers and gave Him a Name that is above every Name. Today He sits upon the Father's throne and someday He will visit this old earth again. He will not come in shame, to be cruelly treated of men, but He will come in glory to rule over men with an almighty hand. Once men judged Him—then He will judge men. Once He was in their hands—then they will be in His hands. Once they cried, "Away with Him" —then He will say, "Depart from Me."

As we see Jesus dying on the Cross, in perfect communion with God, we come to realize that communion with God is not dependent on time and place. There He is on the cross, surrounded by a taunting crowd, suffering untold agony, yet He is in perfect fellowship with the Father. So can we be in perfect communion with God, wherever we be, whatever the circumstances, if our hearts are right with Him.

They threw Daniel into the lions' den, but his heart was right with God. In the middle of the night he had sweet fellowship with the Father. They put the three Hebrew children in the fiery furnace, but they had fellowship with God. The king looked into the furnace and saw not three men, but four, and the fourth was like unto the Son of God. In the fiery furnace, He was present. They put Paul and Silas in the Philippian jail. In the midnight hour, they were not grumbling, but they were singing songs of praise. The Lord was in the cell with them. Yes, if our hearts are right, though sorrow and trouble come, though all the world be against us, we can have fellowship with God.

We can have fellowship with Him in the hour of death—Jesus did. David said, "Though I walk through the valley of the shadow of death, I will fear no evil, for thou art with me." Christ has taken the sting out of death and we need never fear it. Death is nothing but a door. Through it we pass from a land of sorrow and tears to a land where God shall wipe away all tears. Through it we pass from sickness to perfect health— from weakness to perfect strength—from the presence of sin right into the presence of our blessed Saviour. So, when we come down to die, let us have no fears— let us just rest in the everlasting arms of Jesus, and He will take us safely home.

Jesus could say, "Father." Is God your Father? Not unless you have trusted Christ as your Saviour. Jesus said, "I am the way, no man cometh unto the Father but by me." John 1:12—"As many as received him to them gave he the power to become the sons of God." Today some men claim that God is their Father, but they leave Jesus out. This is an insult both to God and to Christ. We never know God as our Father until we know Christ as our Saviour.

What a wonderful thing it is to know that God is our Father! It means that every need shall be supplied; it means comfort in sorrow; it means that He will give assurance when the heart is fainting; it means that He will never let us fall; it means that He will cause all things to work together for our good. It means that at the end of the way He will have His house of many mansions awaiting us. So, as Jesus dies, we see that again He is in sweet and blessed communion with God the Father.

II. HERE WE SEE JESUS SETTING A GOOD EXAMPLE
FOR US

As He yielded Himself to God in the hour of death, so He yielded Himself to God all through His life. He never sought to do His own will, but God's will. He said, "My meat is to do the will of Him that sent me." He said, "I come to do thy will." He said in the Garden, "Not my will, but thine be done." Though it meant suffering and death, He could say, "I am clay in the Heavenly Potter's hands. I have no will of my own, I seek to please Him only."

Men usually die as they live. A certain man in the restaurant business established many eating places across the country. When He came to die those at his bedside leaned over to catch his last words. This is what he said, "Slice the ham thin." This was the one passion of his life—he died as he had lived. So did Jesus. His life was one of committing Himself to God. When He died, He died as He lived. He committed Himself to God.

The only way for a sinner to be saved is to commit himself to God, through Christ. On the Cross Jesus purchased our salvation—now He offers it freely to all men. He says, "The door is open, walk in. Commit thyself wholly unto Me, and I will save you forever." Paul, telling of his experience, said, "I saw the light, I heard a voice, and I was not disobedient to the heavenly vision." He yielded himself to Christ. Later on he could say, "I am persuaded that He is able to keep that which I have committed unto Him against that day." Salvation is a matter of committing oneself to God through Jesus Christ.

When the rich young man came to Jesus, the Saviour said to him, "Go and sell all that you have and give to the poor and come and follow me." He was telling him to turn his back upon his money and to commit himself and his whole life to Christ. The ruler was not willing to do it. He loved his money and was not willing to give it up and trust Christ for all of the future. So he went away sorrowful, to live an empty life, to die a Christless death, and to fill a Christless grave. All of this because he would not commit himself to Christ.

I know some fine people. They are cultured, clean, friendly, kind and good in many ways. But one day they are going to die and they will soon find themselves in the pits of hell. Why? Is it because they are mean and wicked? No, it is because they will not commit their souls to Jesus.

Christians need to make this committal also. They should not be satisfied just to give their souls over to Christ to be saved from hell. They ought to commit their lives to Him, allow Him to sit upon the throne of their hearts and lead them every step of the way. Listen to Psalm 37:5—"Commit thy way unto the Lord; trust also in Him; and He shall bring it to pass."

Paul lived for many things before he came to Christ. When he was converted, he died to all of these things. He said, "I have suffered the loss of all things and count them but refuse, that I might know Christ." When a man is saved, he ought to die to the old life. But that is not enough. Paul said, "I die daily." He died to all of his dreams and desires that he might live wholly for Jesus.

Every day you and I have fresh temptations to give our lives to the things of this world. But every day we should die anew to all that is not pleasing to Christ. We should say in the words of Galatians 2:20—"I am crucified with Christ; nevertheless I live; yet not I, but Christ liveth in me; and the life which I now live in the flesh, I live by the faith of the Son of God, who loved me, and gave himself for me."

So in yielding himself to God in life and in death Jesus set a worthy example for us.

III. WE SEE HERE CHRIST MAKING A FINAL OFFERING FOR SIN

In Old Testament times thousands of priests went through endless ceremonies. Sacrificial animals were brought to the temple; they were slain and their blood was poured into a vessel. The priests would then go into the Holy Place and offer this blood to make atonement for sin. All this was pointing toward the Cross. The slain lamb was a picture of Jesus, the Lamb of God. The blood that was shed was a picture of the precious blood of Christ, which was shed for our sins. Now, as Jesus goes back to the Father, He takes His own blood and offers it for the sins of men. "Father," He said, "men are lost. It is written in thy word that sin must be punished, that a price must be paid for iniquity. With my blood I have come to pay the redemption price for all men." When God looked upon the rich, royal blood of His only begotten Son, which was poured out upon Calvary, He accepted it as the complete price for man's redemption.

It was not the quantity of blood that counted with God, it was the quality. Since it was the blood of heaven's Prince, the blood of Immanuel, the blood of the Fairest among Ten Thousand, the blood of the One Altogether Lovely, God accepted this blood as payment. The blood of bulls and goats and lambs would no longer suffice. Your blood and mine would not avail. But "the blood of Jesus Christ His Son cleanses from all sin." "We are redeemed not by silver and gold, but by the precious blood of the Lamb of God."

When Jesus offered His blood, payment was finally made. No more offerings were necessary—this was enough. The law was satisfied now, the price was finally paid. Let any man come to Christ and get under the blood and God will look upon Him as He looks upon

Jesus Christ. He cannot see your sin through the blood of His Son. Thank God, the price is paid, the debt is settled. God is satisfied. You and I don't have to add anything to what has been done in order to be saved.

> Jesus paid it all,
> All to Him I owe,
> Sin had left a crimson stain,
> He washed it white as snow.

IV. HERE WE FIND THE SAFEST PLACE FOR OUR SOULS

Jesus said, "Into thy hands I commend my spirit." There is the safest place for our souls—in the hands of God. Put your soul today in His keeping and it will be safe forever. Listen to John 10:29—"My Father, which gave them to me, is greater than all; and no man is able to pluck them out of my Father's hand." You may be the weakest Christian in the world, but if you have trusted Christ as your Saviour, you are just as safe as if you had been in heaven a thousand years.

If you say that one can be saved by the power of God and then admit that he can be lost, you are saying that Satan is greater than God. Surely this is not so. God's hand, the hand which created the world, the hand which heaped up the mountains and scooped out the seas, the hand which flung the sun and the moon and the stars into space, the hand which moves men and nations at His will—that hand is the Almighty Hand which will keep us as His own forever.

In Fort Knox, Kentucky, the United States has a great deposit of gold. This gold is buried in the depths of the earth, surrounded by buildings of steel and concrete, and enclosed by steel fences and barbed wire. Soldiers are on guard both day and night. We say that this gold is safe, but I tell you that it is not half as safe as the soul that has leaned upon Jesus for salvation. Before Satan can get one soul away from Christ, he must tear down all the battlements of heaven. He must throw God off His throne, he must conquer Christ and silence Him forever, he must slay all the hosts of angels who serve God day and night. I tell you that this is an impossibility. Thank God for the Cross. Thank God for the Christ who died thereon; thank God for the salvation which He freely gives! Thank God for the heavenly home which awaits us!

Let me ask you a personal question. Is this Christ your Saviour? Are you trusting Him for your salvation? Oh, my friend, don't trust anything else! Don't trust your goodness, your works, your gifts, your church affiliation—just trust Jesus if you want to be saved.

Then you should confess to the world that He is yours. Listen to Romans 10:9, 10—"That if thou shalt confess with thy mouth the Lord Jesus, and shalt believe in thine heart that God hath raised him from the dead, thou shalt be saved. For with the heart man believeth unto righteousness; and with the mouth confession is made unto salvation."

And now we turn away from Calvary, but the shadow of the Cross will hover over us throughout all of time and bless us through all of eternity. We will never forget what happened there. Most of all, we will never forget the Christ who died there in our stead, who arose from the dead, who ascended on high, who is coming back again some day. Because of Him and what He did at Calvary, you and I can be cleansed from our sins, we can pass from the kingdom of darkness into the kingdom of light, we can become the children of God and inherit everlasting life. Glory be to His Name forevermore!

One day a woman fell from a steamer into the muddy

waters of the Mississippi River. A good swimmer leaped in and saved her. Afterward the other women on the steamer tried to minister to her. "Would you like a cup of coffee?" they asked. "No," she replied. Several others asked if they could be of any help to her. Finally one of them said, "What do you want?" And she replied, "I just want to see the man who saved me." When we get to heaven and the angels rush out to welcome us, I am sure that we will say, "I want to see the man who saved me. I want to see Jesus." And, thank God, because of Calvary we can see Him and be with Him forever and forever.